AF470510

'BIG BIRD'

FLYING HIGH

'BIG BIRD'

FLYING HIGH

The Autobiography of

JOEL GARNER

ARTHUR BARKER

A subsidiary of George Weidenfeld and Nicolson Limited
London

FOR GRAN

IN MEMORIAM

Published in Great Britain by
George Weidenfeld & Nicolson Limited
91 Clapham High Street
London SW4 7TA

ISBN 0 213 16955 X

Printed in Great Britain by
Butler & Tanner Ltd, Frome and London

ILLUSTRATIONS

Between pages 56 and 57

Big Bird flying high (*All-Sport*)
With my brother Bob
The house where I grew up (*Barbados Board of Tourism*)
Carter's Gap (*Barbados Board of Tourism*)
Getting established in Barbadian club cricket
A breakthrough into the Barbados team
Under close scrutiny in the nets
Botham and Richards congratulate me (*Patrick Eager*)
More encouragement from Botham (*All-Sport*)
Somerset fans at the Benson and Hedges final (*All-Sport*)
A bear hug for Trevor Gard (*Patrick Eager*)
Lining up the prey
Sometimes it helps to be tall
The 1979 World Cup winners (*Ken Kelly*)
Meeting the Queen at Lord's
It's never easy to find my size

Between pages 120 and 121

Helping out an autograph hunter
The West Indies' touring team, 1984
Keeping the skipper in trim
Bowling to Allan Lamb (*All-Sport*)
Stooping to conquer (*All-Sport*)
Action from the West Indies' tour of Australia, 1984–85
My 200th Test wicket
My wife Heather and daughter Jewel (*Solo Syndication*)
The house in which I now live (*Barbados Board of Tourism*)
At the public meeting of Somerset rebels (*Bristol Press & Picture Agency*)

I still feel attached to the place (*Solo Syndication*)
With my grandmother Editha

The illustrations in this book come from Joel Garner's collection
unless otherwise stated.

ACKNOWLEDGEMENTS

I would like to thank all those who have helped in making this book possible. I drew heavily on *Wisden* and the *West Indies Cricket Annual* to jolt my sometimes flagging memory, and would therefore like to thank the editors of those admirable publications. Keith Holder at *The Nation* provided useful and detailed research. Tony Cozier and Louis Brathwaite produced excellent reports of matches played in the Caribbean which I avidly read. They helped a great deal. Above all, I would like to thank my friend, Harry Eastmond, for all the help he has given in the preparation of what I hope will be an enjoyable book.

1

G rowing up in Barbados, I shared with my friends an over-whelming enjoyment of cricket and the ambition to play for the West Indies. For us, the game was more than a sport. The famous players were our folk heroes; prowess with bat and ball our sign of manhood. Before we could identify England and Australia on a world map, we knew that the MCC and Aussies were our foes. We played cricket of one sort or another almost every day and certainly at every opportunity, determined to become one of those men who appeared to enjoy a superlative life of travel and entertainment. During the fifties and sixties we followed their exploits on the cricket field with much the same enthusiasm, awe, and fidelity that others our age reserved for the Phantom, Rip Kirby and Dick Tracy.

In our games it took little imagination for the transformation to take place from poor black youth to Weekes, Worrell, Sobers or Walcott. A Gary Sobers with right-handed pull would loft a tennis ball high in the air. Day after day, a skinny, bandy-legged, bare-footed Wes Hall or Charlie Griffith would hurl harmless thunderbolts at a black Geoff Boycott, an ebony John Edrich or Colin Cowdrey. In this fantasy world, African Lawrys, Stackpoles and Davidsons abounded. If we read or heard reports that Graham McKenzie got six wickets on any day, the next morning every child with a marathon run-up would be Mc-Kenzie; and if Dexter got runs, the neighbourhood teemed with Lord Teds.

We ate, drank, and slept cricket. It was a religion that made us forget that Sundays were for church going. We often made our parents angry when its invisible magnet, whose power sur-passed the church's, drew us to the playing fields and alleys. In those days, West Indies cricketers played the game in a way that commentators usually called 'calypso cricket'. They seemed to hold the result of a particular contest to be of secondary importance; the satisfaction of players and spectators being the primary consideration. That was the kind of cricket we wanted to play: cricket for fun.

From about the age of ten I had two goals in life: to become a policeman and to play cricket well. I imagined that the perfect life would consist of pounding the beat during the week and playing cricket for a local team on weekends, having of course made the West Indies team on a couple of occasions. In my dreams my spare time would be spent swimming in the clear blue waters of the Caribbean.

That was my ambition until, one day in February 1977, I accepted for the first time that my goal was within reach and not merely an idle dream. It happened during the President's XI match in the West Indies against a touring team from Pakistan. This game is usually an invitational charity affair whose main purpose is to acclimatize visiting players to Caribbean conditions before they play more important matches. The touring sides use such opportunities for batting practice, so it is rare for the games to end with an outright result. The most that could be said for them is that they give the selectors an opportunity to have a close look at promising youngsters or to check the form of any established player going through a bad spell. Normally the West Indies side is picked from among those players who performed well in the annual Shell Shield games between the islands, and the team is more or less decided before the President's XI match. Consequently, the game is not considered one of the important fixtures on the itinerary.

By 1977 I had spent three years feeling that I deserved to play as a regular for the Barbados team, and although I was always on the verge of selection I repeatedly suffered the pain of rejection when I was left out. On a couple of occasions before I finally made it I thought that I had been unfortunate, victimized because I was not then playing First Division cricket. Considering its size of only 166 square miles, it is amazing that Barbados produces so many talented world-class players. The Barbados team is like a select club into which entry is particularly difficult. During the early seventies, Barbados had a high number of good fast bowlers, even by its own standards.

For a while it looked as though the only place that I might find myself at national level would be limited to being twelfth and thirteenth man.

In 1975 and early 1976, I watched a lot of cricket at that level; but, apart from net practice, I played very little. I spent a great deal of time reading the sports pages in the local press and following the misfortunes of the West Indies team in Australia in the press and on radio. I became more and more frustrated at not being able to do anything to help myself secure a place in the Barbados side.

The 1975–6 tour of Australia was an almost total disaster for our team. Some sports writers had even gone as far as suggesting that the team was incapable of competing against the top international sides. One Australian reporter had written:

> The West Indies cricketers are becoming an embarrassment. The sooner the sixth test is over and the West Indies disastrous tour is over the better it will be for everyone. The Windies will be able to slink home and prepare for tests against India and England, opponents more their calibre.

During the last test, another writer expressed this opinion:

> They should open the gates free at the Melbourne Cricket Ground for the rest of this tragically one-sided sixth test between Australia and the West Indies. Surely the Australian Board is in danger of infringing the Trade Practices Act on the score of false and misleading representation because this simply isn't a test match.

Only Clive Lloyd, who had led the defeated side, offered a glimmer of hope. He said, 'We are tired, especially some of our older players. Our rebuilding for the future must include some of the younger promising players.'

I certainly wanted to be part of that rebuilding process; but I couldn't see how I could make it. Talking with others, I realized that I was not the only West Indian who felt badly because the West Indies were beaten by the Australians. The performances were bad, but ours was far from being a mediocre team. But there was something wrong, something missing. Perhaps it was simply the lack of professionalism. Because of the poor performance by the West Indies, Australia looked even better than they really were. They had good cricketers it is true, and also a little bit of extra help. This was proved when

Pakistan drew a three-match series against them immediately following the West Indies tour. At that time, Pakistan were considered one of the weakest sides in the international arena.

The West Indies team regained its lost prestige with a convincing win over England in 1976; but the real challenge was always to beat the Australians. West Indian cricketers have always thought the Australians to be much tougher opponents than the English. It is always a thrill to win against England, but the acid test is to beat Australia. The men in the baggy caps were known to give no quarter, and expected none.

The Pakistanis were due to tour the West Indies in 1977. This became something for me to look forward to. If we could beat the Pakistanis, we would be on the way to a recovery. I thought that the competition would be good. It was an exciting time for me; but I didn't dare think that I might get picked for the team.

But at the beginning of 1977 circumstances changed dramatically. All of the leading fast bowlers on the West Indies team, who had wreaked havoc in England the previous summer, were injured early in the year. Andy Roberts had broken down while playing Sheffield Shield cricket; and although official reports stated that he had fully recovered from back problems, a contradictory message that he was not at all fit whizzed along the cricket grapevine. Michael Holding had not announced whether he would be available for the entire Pakistan tour. It was rumoured that he had begun a degree programme at the University of the West Indies and had not made a firm decision whether to continue his education or to play cricket. Many an opening batsman would later regret that he did not finally choose university. In addition, Michael had suffered a shoulder injury in a Jamaica–Barbados Shell Shield game and had missed an important match against Trinidad. Wayne Daniel had not played for Barbados against Guyana because of sore ribs. In our first game against Jamaica his bowling had not been up to the usual standard that he would have wanted.

Because of these injuries to established players, a slight chance arose that I could be picked – if I performed reasonably well in the games leading up to the test matches. And it did not bother me that I might last only as long in the team as the established fast-bowling stars were unavailable. I thought that even if I was lucky enough to be picked, I would be dropped when the other bowlers recovered.

The day after the Pakistanis arrived in the Caribbean, Barbados began a game against Trinidad in the local Shield competition. I think I had been selected to play mainly because Vanburn Holder withdrew from the side. The match was played at Queen's Park Oval where the wicket has a well-deserved reputation for favouring spin bowling from quite early in a game. It has been alleged for a long time that Barbados and West Indies batsmen are suspect against spin bowling. It was therefore not surprising that at the end of the first day's play we had been dismissed for a paltry 145. The spinner Inshan Ali had taken 5 wickets for 44 runs. In their innings, the Trinidadians mustered 111 for 3. I had bowled accurately but not outstandingly and at the close had figures of 9–1–35–1.

On the second day, we managed to bowl out the Trinidadians for 271. I had taken five wickets, four of them clean bowled, and had figures of 18.3–1–64–5. In fact, our score would have been a much more challenging proposition had it not been for a sixth wicket partnership of 134 between Larry Gomes (90) and Bernard Julien (73), both of whom were talented cricketers and in the West Indies side.

In our second innings we did only a little better against the spin than we had on the first day. This time, the day's play ended with us on 101 for 4. The next day, however, we crumbled to 246 all out; and the Trinidadians, needing 121 runs to win, were 98 for 3. Trinidad predictably won the game on the final day. I took three of the five second innings' wickets which had fallen, including that of Larry Gomes who had given us so much trouble in their first innings. My figures were 13.1–2–36–3.

We lost that Shield game to Trinidad, but because we had won a couple of earlier matches we were still tied for first place in the overall standings with the Combined Islands team led by Viv Richards. I was disappointed with our batting performance and the fact that we'd lost, but I was satisfied with my bowling. It is likely that the eight wickets that I took in that lost game secured my place in the side which met the Pakistanis in the President's XI match. In addition, my chances of inclusion in the West Indies team increased with the announcement on the day before the scheduled start of the game, that Wayne Daniel, a certainty to play if fit, would be out of cricket for at least six months. Wayne, who had worked his heart out in England, was suffering from a crushed vertebra.

The playing field at Castries, St Lucia, where the President's XI match was to be played, is not a famous ground; but its quaint pavilion and location make it an ideal spot for a friendly game. The field itself is on a plateau bordered on one side by verdant mountains and on the other the rooftops of the city stand above the shimmering blue Caribbean in a multi-coloured mosaic. Bowlers in the West Indies are used to bowling in small grounds, and when I first saw the field I was more anxious about how I would perform against reputable batsmen.

I would have loved the game to have been played in Barbados, because by that time I had become accustomed to the atmosphere at Kensington Oval and I knew that the local fans would have given me all their support. As it turned out, the St Lucians welcomed us with open arms, provided excellent hospitality and whole-heartedly supported the team. Yet I still had recurring visions of me bowling all day against batsmen who knocked the ball all over the ground without as much as offering a chance. That Majid Khan and his crew brought glowing reputations with them did nothing to relieve the pressure.

As soon as the match itself began, my fears evaporated. I took a Pakistani opener's wicket when he tried to force a half volley and missed. Preparing to bowl to Sadiq Mohammad, I walked back to my marker and thought that I would attempt a yorker – at that time the delivery that brought me the most success. I had bowled hundreds of them. I had no idea that there would be anything special about this particular one. On reaching the marker and turning around, I saw that the batsman was ready: his compact figure appeared totally relaxed. He scarcely tapped his bat at the crease, as most batsmen do. I bent my back, began to run in, and an unusual surge of energy coursed through my body with each step I took. Aware that I was moving smoothly, I increased the speed of my run-up and decided to bowl as fast as I could. When I straightened up a few steps before reaching the crease, my back did not jerk, throwing me off-stride as had sometimes happened in the past. I leapt into my delivery stride and sent my out-stretched left arm as high as I could into the air. Sadiq moved his right foot slightly forward. Then my right arm went up high – a height from which I am sure Sadiq had never before seen a ball coming.

He raised his bat to a point just about level with the top of the stumps. The yorker was a delivery that I constantly practised and I had come to specialize in it. When I saw how he had raised his bat, I knew that I had him. His bat was not coming down as straight as it should have been. Angled across the line of flight, it barely brushed the ball which swept past and crashed into the stumps behind him.

My arms flew up in excitement. I let go a spontaneous, excited shout. I felt filled with joy and excitement. There are few emotions experienced during a game of cricket equal to that of a bowler's at the moment he has hit a batsman's stumps. I do not think that the well-executed stroke or the reflex catch give the same satisfaction or genuine sensation of triumph. Many games and years later, the thrill and excitement of that moment still remain with me. I knew then that I would become a full professional cricketer.

When my yorker broke through Sadiq's defences, I felt great confidence in my abilities, not only as a local fast bowler but also as one who could dismiss top-ranking batsmen. In spite of what others had told me of my potential, it was only in that instant that I honestly began to feel that I was a potential West Indies player and that I might even do reasonably well as a member of the squad. Because, had not Sadiq and the rest of his team batted successfully against Lillee and Thomson, then considered the two best fast bowlers in the world?

They say that when you are about to die your whole life passes before you. I don't know whether an instant can take in the experiences of an even a short lifetime. But I do know that in that single moment, the pain of practice, the disappointment and boredom of waiting, the depression of having been overlooked when I felt that I could have done better than some who had been chosen instead and the desire of a life's ambition to play cricket for the West Indies, all came together and I felt justified. A strange consciousness of my own maturity suddenly came over me, as if I had successfully completed my days and months of waiting in preparation.

I was one of two novice fast bowlers that fate and an unpredictable combination of factors had determined would be chosen for the President's game. We both knew that the selectors would be watching us closely for possible inclusion in the West Indies side for the first test. The other bowler was Colin Croft whose career after that game was to parallel my own almost exactly until very recently, and who before the game had experienced similar apparent oversight in the selection process at the national level. Colin had played Shell Shield cricket when he was very young (in 1972 or 1973) and had at one time seriously considered giving up the game because he felt constantly overlooked for selection. He had always been a bowler who provided the batsman with little chance of making a big score. His unorthodox approach to the wicket and his ability to move the ball both ways off the wicket made batting against him, at best, difficult. Before this first game in which we were to play together, we wished each other good luck and both expressed the hope that we would do well enough to play in the tests.

On the first day, the two of us, working almost constantly in tandem, bowled out the Pakistanis for 203 runs. Colin and I engaged in a friendly rivalry for wickets that could not possibly have pleased the batsmen. We knew what we were playing for. Young and relatively inexperienced, we bowled on that first day as if it was a one-day game. We were fast, fit, furious, and uncannily accurate. I know for my part that I fully expected every delivery to take a wicket. I think that Colin did the same. We didn't bother to set up the batsmen. We bowled expecting to get a wicket with every ball. If we felt that a yorker would do the job, then we bowled, or tried to bowl, yorkers until one got through. Our bowling figures reflect the closeness of the competition between us. I bowled 16 overs with 6 maidens and took 3 wickets for 46 runs. Colin took 4 wickets for 43 runs off 16 overs with 6 maidens.

All the team members knew that the selectors had chosen Kallicharran as captain of the side so that they could see if he had fully recovered from a shoulder injury that had caused a patch of poor form. On the second day, Kalli dispelled any doubts about his form or his shoulder by lambasting the Pakistani bowling for 134 runs. Our team made 380. When the disconsolate Pakistanis batted a second time, Colin and I again presented them with problems they could not handle. I got Sadiq out for the second time, but on this occasion the dismissal did not give me half the thrill that it had in the first innings. He was easily caught in the covers by Larry Gomes. Colin also got two quick wickets and, at the end of the day's play, the visitors were 41 for 3 after having been 6 runs for 3 wickets at one stage.

On the final day of the game, Colin and I quickly cleaned up the Pakistanis. We bowled them out for 113 runs, to win by an innings. We bowled as if our futures, our hopes, our dreams, depended upon success. Colin again held the edge over me. He took 6 for 66 while I got the other 4 for 40. We celebrated together afterwards and we were both sure that we had done better than had been expected and that we had forced the selectors to consider us seriously.

When I had bowled Sadiq in the first innings, I had convinced myself that I would be a test player; but after the game, given Colin's better overall performance, I began to doubt whether the test in Barbados would be the one in which I would make it. I felt that if the selectors picked two new fast bowlers, then I would play; but if they chose only one, the place would most likely go to Colin. His angled approach to the crease, double-pump action before delivery, and extremely high speed made him virtually unplayable. Colin was never the smoothest, most rhythmical fast bowler; but he was effective. Batsmen never seemed to know where to position themselves to be in line for his deliveries. The Pakistanis had made a few more runs off him than they had off me; but he had taken more wickets.

As the days immediately following the President's XI game passed, my uncertainty about actually being chosen for the test grew; but I remained very happy about my performance in St Lucia. The more I thought about the situation, the more I remembered how close I had been to selection in the past and the more I felt that I needed an ace up my sleeve if it came down to a choice between myself and Colin. I assured myself that I did have such an ace: the following and only game the Pakistanis would play before the first test would be the one against Barbados, and I would have a chance to perform for the selectors once again. Since Colin played for Guyana, I wouldn't have to bother about him blasting them out. I had found it easy to bowl against the tourists in St Lucia, and I looked forward to meeting them in Barbados with the local fans supporting me. I felt that if I could get a handful of wickets in the first innings and a couple in the second for only a few runs then I would be certain of a place even if the selectors chose only one new bowler for the test.

No one could have been happier than I was on the morning of the game between Barbados and Pakistan. I awoke earlier than usual and answered a knock at the door at about eight o'clock when about six of my buddies from Carter's Gap came to get me. I had played with them all my life, and they had always followed me from ground to ground if they were within walking distance. They wanted to go to Kensington Oval with me and we took the bus. They were even more excited than I was. As we travelled on the bus, they constantly came up with some of the most incredible bowling figures. 'Mosquito' went so far as to suggest that if the Pakistanis batted first I would get all ten wickets. 'Diode' said that that was being unrealistic. He was certain, nonetheless, that I would get some of the wickets.

When I got to the ground and had a look at the wicket, a thought that had been in the back of my mind but that I had not consciously considered struck me. Since the St Lucia game, I had thought of Kensington Oval in terms of the local fans and me being accusomed to the surroundings. What now came to mind was what every cricketer who has ever played at Kensington knows: there were few, if any, better batting strips in the West Indies at that time. The wicket was flat and bare. Not a blade of grass showed on the surface. I remember thinking that a wicket like that could only be prepared under instructions, but I quickly dismissed the feeling of dejection and the negative thoughts that caused it. After all, wasn't I the Joel Garner who had taken eighteen wickets in three Shield matches already that year? Wasn't I one of the heroes of Castries?

Perhaps I was; but Kensington was not St Lucia. In a short while I saw that the difference between the two wickets was vast. At Majid Khan I bowled what I thought would be two of the most lethal bouncers only to watch the ball dispatched to the square leg boundary from pull shots made with lots of time to spare. This was to be only the beginning of my grief. Our fielding was atrocious: seven catches were dropped on the first day, and Pakistan finished with a score of 280 for 4.

After a night in which I frequently awoke in fear of being out of my depth as far as 'serious' cricket was concerned, I returned to Kensington for a second day that was hardly more successful than the first. Pakistan finally declared at 443 for 9, and I had scored the first of many tons in first-class cricket as a bowler, capturing 2 for 104 in 27 overs. In comparison, Vanburn Holder, a dear friend and at the time the best old-ball bowler anywhere, who could make the ball move about on any type of wicket, also took 2 wickets; but at the cost of only 61 runs. In the time left on the second day Barbados managed to score 188 for 1, and Desmond Haynes partly made up for the catches he had dropped by scoring an unbeaten 118. His brilliant batting could in no way change the figures of those bowlers whose catches he had put down. Perhaps I am being too harsh on Dessie. He had apparently suffered an attack of nervousness in the field, most likely caused by the circumstances of his selection for the game: he had gained his place at the last moment after Gordon Greenidge had withdrawn because of an injury.

On the third day, we declared at 419 for 7. Haynes added a further 18 runs to his overnight score and David Murray scored a useful 57. Pakistan made a furious 65 without loss in even time after the tea interval. Between them, the two teams had scored 927 runs in three days, and although this would have pleased the fans who enjoy watching batsmen going for their strokes and making runs, it did nothing at all for my confidence. At this point the game appeared certain to end in a draw because the Pakistanis did not have the bowling power to get through our batting in one day on a wicket that played so evenly. All that was left for me to do was to try and bowl as well as I could and get a couple of wickets to prevent the selectors from forgetting my performance in St Lucia. I concentrated on maintaining a good length and, in two spells of six overs, I took 1 wicket for 28 runs. I was reasonably satisfied because the Pakistanis finally made 240 for 8 declared. Although Vannie Holder had taken 1 for 52 off the same 12 overs, no one could have been fooled by such a comparison because the difference between my ability and his was like the difference between chalk and cheese. In any case, I felt chastened but reassured as Barbados placidly made 99 for 2 and the game ended in a tame draw.

That first serious game against a touring team made me reflect upon cricket's uncertainty. The Barbados–Pakistan game was one in which I felt the presence of some mischievous force. In addition, my experiences during the game brought to light one of its aspects that I was to reflect upon on many occasions in years to come: fast bowling is not only a relationship between batsman and bowler. It is at the very least a four way interaction between bowler, batsman, fielders and wicket. Often this last element, which might sometimes be the most important, is overlooked by players and fans alike; some of whom should know better. Only the very best fast bowlers can bother world-class batsmen on easy wickets, and Kensington, for the duration of the Barbados–Pakistan match, was so peaceful it should have been awarded a Nobel Prize.

Cricket is often referred to as the game of glorious uncertainties. I consider what happened to me in the space of those two weeks a demonstration of the unpredictability not only of the game itself but also of players' careers. Not even this realization, however, could deter me from my intention to play test cricket. I tried to put the last game behind me; and hoped that the selectors would do likewise and, forgetting the rather ordinary performance, include me in the test match team.

For the game starting on Friday 18 February 1977, the West Indian selectors faced one of those decisions that would affect the structure of West Indies cricket for a long time to come. They could field a side that included four quickies. This was, at the time, unheard of in world cricket. During the comeback series against England we had played, at most, three genuine fast bowlers. Of course, the idea of playing a test match under such conditions and without a seamer or recognized spin bowler was unheard of and would have been suicidal.

When the team was announced, I was overjoyed to have been included in the thirteen from whom the final eleven would be chosen. Holder, Croft and Roberts were also picked. The only specialist spinner was Jumadeen from Trinidad. To play all four fast bowlers appeared risky since it apparently unbalanced the side, both in terms of batting depth and in the ability to get the Pakistanis out should the wicket favour spin in the closing stages of the game. Such a policy would also depend to a great extent upon the gamble of the toss and upon fielding first in order to take advantage of the wicket when it would be at its fastest.

I think that mainly at Clive Lloyd's instigation, the selectors bit the bullet and chose all four fast bowlers. Perhaps they took the decision for tactical reasons because Roberts, who had to be chosen on ability, did not appear to be in peak form. Whatever the case, it led to consequences that could not have been foreseen at the time. In the normal team, the batsmen were supposed to get the runs and the bowlers were supposed to get the opposing team out. A team with four fast bowlers could easily run into trouble if it were to lose four or five quick wickets. Fast bowlers would have to make runs, not only by slogging, but through an intelligent stay at the crease. What the selection of four fast bowlers meant, if the strategy was to be successful, was that the bowlers would have to develop a different attitude to batting. We were expected to bat down to number eleven. There was no longer room in the side for 'tail-end' batsmen. Much of the West Indies success over the years following the first test against Pakistan in 1977 can be attributed to the significant contributions that bowlers have made with the bat. Every West Indian fast bowler has made fifty runs in a first-class game, and Malcolm Marshall has often come close to making centuries.

The experiment of playing four fast bowlers, initiated by force of circumstance and the Caribbean flair on the cricket field for flouting tradition in favour of the bold move, resulted in the development of a stronger side. Such a team, confronting the more normally-structured sides, would have to be odds-on favourites to win.

Another important feature of the West Indian game followed from this decision to play four fast bowlers. In the West Indies, fast bowlers usually come from the lower classes and playing cricket represents for them a means of bettering themselves and a chance for social recognition. They are therefore usually a bit more aggressive than batsmen. A team with four fast bowlers could therefore turn out to be more competitive. Wes Hall, our manager in Australia, once told the team a story. During a tour of England the West Indies had given some county team about twenty or so runs to win. The captain called Wes before he had bowled his first over and said, 'Okay, Blues, now let's not play around. Bowl a couple of full tosses and long hops. Let these guys get the runs and let us get out of here.'

Wes agreed and was marking out a short run-up when his bowling partner, Charlie Griffith, came over and asked, 'What did the skipper tell you?'

'Oh, he said bowl a couple of full tosses and let them get the runs,' Wes answered.

'What?' Charlie exclaimed. 'You must be joking. Bowl a maiden over.'

Wes was surprised. 'Charlie,' he said, 'don't you see that the people only have twenty runs to win? We don't have a hope in hell and I don't intend to prolong the agony.'

'Bowl a maiden over,' Charlie repeated, and strode away.

Wes said, in his jovial way, that he decided to do what Charlie had asked him. In the space of the following two overs from Charlie, two batsmen got out and a third retired hurt. At which point the skipper, always the gentleman, took him off and assigned him a fielding position at deep fine leg from which he watched remorsefully as the county side won the game.

This story might well have been untrue. Wes has a deserved reputation for embellishing his tales. Perhaps he told it merely to demonstrate what fast bowling aggression was all about, but it shows quite clearly the kind of hostility some West Indian fast bowlers can generate. Lest anyone fool themselves, I should point out that the grace of Michael Holding and of Wes Hall himself in his playing days, only hides the same kind of hostility; it doesn't replace it. A team with four such members must have a greater will to win than sides led by gentlemen batsmen who exchange pleasantries during a match or, instead of chasing the ball when it is struck by one of their counterparts on the opposing side, stand and applaud. For these kinds of players, cricket is an arena in which they may showcase their talents, and not a hard-fought job at which one earns a living.

At the beginning of my first test match, I doubted that I could showcase any hostility real or imagined. The wicket was very like that of the previous week when I was stroked for a ton. I didn't really want to bowl, and my eagerness did not increase when the Pakistani openers casually collected 66 runs from 13 overs off our strike bowlers. Majid especially caressed the short-pitched delivery with such ease that Roberts appeared to be bowling at half pace. Sadiq produced flowing off and cover drives that sped across the grass. To add to our general dis-comfort, Vannie Holder, my room-mate, pulled up with a ham-string injury after he had bowled only a couple of overs.

Vannie's injury upset me as much as if it had been my own. It appears that someone always gains from another's misfortune, and in this case I benefitted because Vannie's inability to bowl meant that I was brought into the attack more quickly than I otherwise would have been. I therefore had a chance to bowl with a newer ball, which improved my chances of getting a wicket. I felt sorry for Vannie. He had been my friend for a very long time and we got along together excep-tionally well. He taught me how to bowl an effective outswinger when my stock-in-trade was a fast inswinger. He gave me refresher courses in gripping the ball, keeping the shine, and cutting the old ball. I knew that, in a team that could call on the number of fast bowlers that we had, it was dangerous, career-wise, to be injured; especially when playing in the West Indies.

However, I don't think that how I felt about Vannie affected the way I bowled that day. After realizing that Sadiq expected me to bowl a full-length at him continually in an attempt to york him, as I had done in St Lucia, I gave him a bouncer that I released with every ounce of my strength. The speed, the length and the angle caught him by surprise and he attempted a hook while badly out of position. The ball lobbed gently to Colin Croft at mid-on. As my team-mates surrounded and congratulated me on claiming my first test wicket, I noticed the excited expression on Colin's face. He said, as he handed the ball back to me, 'Leh we do it again, boy.'

I felt that it was some kind of sign that Colin had taken the catch. I sensed that he felt something similar: we both expected a repeat of St Lucia. By teatime, Rashid had been caught by Kallicharran and Colin had claimed his first test wicket by totally beating the surprised Mustaq Mohammad and had him caught behind for a duck. During the tea break, in the dressing room the skipper told us that we were going to miss Vannie and that things were going to be a bit harder. We would have to carry some more of the responsibility. He asked if I felt up to an extended spell until late in the afternoon. Up to it? He must have been crazy. Now I would have bowled unchanged from both ends, if he had asked me.

I was trying to put into effect all that I had learned about bowling up to that point. It paid off when Majid Khan, after a splendid 88, during which he looked as though he was sure to make a hundred, played over a straight yorker and lost his leg stump. I was overjoyed; never more than when I looked towards the pavilion and saw Vannie's broad, beaming smile clearly distinguishable sixty yards away.

When Majid got out, the score was 186 for 4. I soon produced an inswinger that kept low and Javed Miandad, caught unawares, was struck directly in front of the stumps after he had scored 2. Because of Javed's reputation, I was extremely pleased at getting him out. He had made a double and single century against New Zealand just before coming to the Caribbean. At the team meeting he had been one of the batsmen that our bowlers were cautioned to keep a close and watchful eye on. Other bowlers appeared to have been warned about his potential too, for he made only 60 runs in his first seven innings in the West Indies.

In the spell after tea, I was rewarded with a haul of 2 valuable wickets for 24 runs. Far from being contained under 250 runs as I had expected, Pakistan had reached 269 for 6 by the end of the day. That they managed such a score could only have been caused by the intervention of Crickus,* that mischievous spirit that confounds predictions about cricket and with whom, for some unknown reason, Wasim Raja had found favour. Wasim, who at close of play had scored 31 runs, had been so lucky that he should have bought a couple of lottery tickets that day. He constantly played dangerously close to balls pitched outside his off stump without edging. When he did, the ball dropped tantalizingly in front of the slip fielders, carried over their heads, or flashed beyond their reach. He spent three quarters of an hour that afternoon like a man playing Russian

* Crickus: the god of fate in cricket.

roulette with five bullets in a gun and repeatedly pulling the trigger on the single empty chamber. Often when Crickus so protects a player, he reveals his intention at an early stage: Wasim had been dropped off the very first ball he faced.

In spite of the combination of Crickus and Wasim, Colin and I were satisfied with our performances on the first day of our debut test match. I finished the day with 3 wickets for 77 off 25 overs, and Colin had 2 for 51 off 19 overs. On the other hand, Roberts bowled far below his best and had taken no wicket for 85 off 20 overs. This was no reflection on his ability. Andy Roberts was definitely one of the very best fast bowlers I have played with or against. That evening, Colin and I shared the firm expectation that we would once again have the Pakistanis on the run the following day. Neither of us could imagine them scoring more than 300 runs. I went to bed cheerful and relaxed.

The second day began just as Colin and I had expected; but through no effort of ours. Roberts came up with a beauty of a delivery in his first ball of the second over and Imran Khan flicked it straight to me at backward short leg, where I accepted the sharp catch. Saleem Altaf then gave each bowler grounds for the greatest optimism before he was lbw to a faster ball for 19. When Kallicharran took a nice running catch at backward square leg to dismiss Sarfraz Nawaz off Foster's bowling, we thought that the Pakistani innings would be over in a couple of minutes.

Enter Crickus, the demon that makes cricket such a glorious game. Apparently dissatisfied with the extent to which he had teased us the previous afternoon, he now began a full-scale onslaught on our sense of proportion and justice. Wasim, growing in confidence and accepting the grace that had been bestowed upon him, sprayed our bowling to all parts of the ground. By the time that Colin eventually broke the charm by getting Bari out lbw to the kind of wicked delivery that only he seems capable of producing, the Pakistanis had scored 435 runs and Wasim Raja had been left undefeated on 117. We had about an hour and a half left to bat towards the close of the second day and our batsmen proceeded with some caution. We lost our two openers in scoring 109 runs. Indies 109 for 2.

On the third day, our batsmen appeared determined to hand

the advantage to the Pakistanis before Lloyd and Murray added 151 for the sixth wicket, the latter only getting out in the first over after tea. We were 334 for 6 when I went to the wicket to join Lloyd. In a conversation in the middle of the wicket, he asked me if I was nervous and I told him that I wasn't. He said, 'Okay, then try to hold on.' I responded almost immediately by playing a sweet square drive, the memory of which I relish to this day. After a couple more full-blooded strokes, the skipper said to me, 'Hey, Bird, you're looking good.'

No one can upstage a master. Lloyd played a captain's innings of the greatest power and magnificence before square cutting a catch to point when he had scored 157. I became last man out forty minutes before close of play after making 43 runs, including 8 fours. We were all out for 421.

When Majid and Sadiq scored 18 runs in the final period on the third day, and Pakistan held a lead of 32 with two full days of cricket left, a draw seemed inevitable. Early on the fourth day though, when I took two catches off Colin's bowling and Roberts got two other wickets, the Pakistanis seemed nervous at 108 for 4. By lunch, the situation had not improved for them. Colin had taken four wickets and Roberts had two; the tourists were 113 for 6.

After the interval, a little luck came my way and I got Imran out to an unexpectedly good catch by Fredericks in the gully. Then I bowled Salim. Roberts pitched in by having Sarfraz caught behind. The Pakistanis had lost nine wickets for 158 which, with their 14-run lead in the first innings, meant that we had to get 173 to win. A victory, with a day to spare, looked likely.

You guessed it. Of all the things that go to make cricket the unpredictable game that it is, the last pair sticking is the most exasperating. And the Pakistani last pair stuck. Wasim Raja and Wasim Bari provided Pakistan with their best last-wicket stand in test cricket. They made 131 runs in about two hours with the sort of good fortune that most gamblers would give an arm for. Wasim Bari, rescued from drowning in the sea off the team's hotel the day before, made 60 runs; but he was luckless compared to Raja, who had chances at 9, 46, 50, and 54 but who scored 71 runs that were a continuation in every respect of his Russian roulette performance of the first innings.

We were left with 306 runs to win the match, and just over an hour's play on the fourth day. Gordon Greenidge holed out to long leg off Sarfraz's bowling when the score was 12, and Viv Richards with Roy Fredericks batted cautiously through to the end when we were 41 for 1 with the game delicately balanced.

The last day of the first test match between Pakistan and the West Indies at Kensington Oval during the 1977 series presented the spectacle of cricket at its most tense and gripping. Fortune changed hands frequently during the game, and the final day's play brought an appropriate climax to a match that I always remember as definitive of the sort of game cricket is. On that morning, Richards batted with application, intelligence and skill. Admirably supported by Fredericks' defensive play, he had taken the score to 129 at lunch and our victory – not for the first time in the game – appeared a certainty. By the tea interval, Richards had departed after scoring 92 runs, Fredericks had gone for 52, Lloyd for 11 and Foster for 2. Of the established batsmen only Kallicharran remained.

The Pakistani strategy of slowing the game down reduced Kalli to scoring nine runs in just over two hours. When he was finally out to a stroke that was an expression of his desire to push the pace along, I was immediately greeted by a delivery from Saleem that never raised more than two inches between hitting the ground and striking my stumps. Murray was caught in the next over, and we were left with Croft, Roberts and the injured Holder to save the game. For the last two hours of this incredible game, the hunter became the hunted. For half an hour and for twelve of the mandatory last twenty overs Vannie batted like a master with Roberts. With Murray as his runner, his defensive batting could have been recorded for coaching text books. With as many as nine fielders crouching around him, he repeatedly pushed forward with a straight bat that sent the ball instantly into the ground. It took the second new ball with eight overs left in the game, before he could be dismissed; and then Croft joined Roberts in a stone-walling job that robbed the Pakistanis of victory.

The first test match in which I had played ended with several hundred spectators swarming onto the field to salute and congratulate their heroes. I had taken six wickets in the match and scored an important 43 runs. The game itself had been a memorable one with first one side then the other taking command. The crowds on the field shouted for the players to come onto the balcony. I heard them shout, 'Garner.' I heard them shout, 'Bird.' I was flying high.

2

The route, from my birthplace to the moment when I looked over the rails of the players' pavilion at Kensington Oval and acknowledged the cheers of the spectators of an exciting test match in which I had made some contribution, was winding and sometimes tortuous. It began in Enterprise, Christ Church, Barbados on the 16 December 1952. Barbadians call every group of houses on the small island a village. Enterprise was not, when I was born, a village by any other standards; but rather a scattering of houses among fields of sugar cane. The house in which I was born, located at the top of a marl lane running down to the beach where a lighthouse stood, was a modest, grey structure similar to others in the neighbourhood. Most of them were semi-detached, twin-peaked wooden buildings with a flat-topped smaller structure to the rear where the kitchen was usually located.

I was the first of two sons of Myrna Garner and Hutson King. My younger brother, Adrian 'Bob' Garner, was a constant companion and partner in mischief and frivolity from the time he could walk. Barbados in the 1950s was a tightly-structured class society reflecting all the social rigidity of plantation communities the world over. Education and emigration were the only legitimate means of upward mobility available to poor Blacks. Many Bajans (as the local people call themselves) took advantage of the liberal immigration policies then existing in the United States, Britain and Canada, to improve their lot and support families by sending back monthly cheques and packages to relatives at home. While Bob and I were still very young, our parents migrated to Canada and the United States and we were left in the care of our grandparents.

In addition to our grandparents Edith and Vincent, we shared the house with our aunts Carmen and Jean, and uncles John and Edwin. Gran was the head of the household which she ran with a firm hand. Grandfather was the source of unbelievably solid folk wisdom and a keen wit. He often caught us out with all sorts of practical jokes. My family was caring and protective, and Aunt Carmen and I grew particularly close. Bob and I could turn to the family with any problem that we faced in our childhood. They showered us with love, tenderness, compassion and understanding; but also stood no nonsense when we tried to misbehave. In spite of what our parents' surnames might suggest, we had more than our fair share of parental authority.

My family tended a small kitchen garden beside the house from which we got enough vegetables for our needs and for others in the village. Gran also raised chickens, pigs, goats and sheep in our backyard, and I became partly responsible for them from an early age.

The people of Enterprise were poor; but we never considered ourselves underprivileged in any way. We ate properly and had clean clothes to wear. We might not have enjoyed the more outlandish luxuries of the day; but then we never looked for anything that we knew we could not get.

My brother and I established friendships in Enterprise that have lasted to this day. Stephen and Neville Clarke went to church with us when we could not evade Gran or their grand-parents. St Clair Pinder was the clever one amongst us. He came up with many of the nicknames that have stuck. We called him 'Ponnerts'. Another two friends were known as 'Brambles' and 'Sinkie'. Then there was 'Mullaback', 'Jenkins', after the mail house, 'Mosquito', 'Saga', 'Ladau', 'Diode', and 'Bamma'. In addition to these, my family had seven cousins: Mary, Andrew, Esther, Adina, Collin, Grace and Amelia. Every week Gran used to send me to Silver Sands with garden produce for my Aunt Burke. Then my aunt would send back what she thought we didn't have at home. We grew up a very close group of friends and family until we finished school and started to work, or migrate to the United States. There was also Andy, with whom I argued almost constantly, and 'Giant', 'Sharkie', 'McD' and 'Landcat'.

With them, Bob and I learned to play cricket in the main road between the cane fields, while at home Uncle Edwin tried to give us some pointers. He insisted that it was a game to be enjoyed, but also one through which we could grow. He constantly said that cricket was like life. I didn't fully understand what he was trying to say at the time, but I didn't need much convincing that it was a game that I ought to learn to play.

The popularity of cricket as the sport played among young boys in Barbados probably has something to do with the history and geography of the island. Cricket is, if nothing else, an English sport. Barbados is the only Caribbean island that, once settled by those English who were seeking fortunes from the slave trade and sugar manufacture, has had no other colonial master. Today, there are still people who call the island 'little England'.

Bob and I became involved in this most English of sports as a matter of course. We played a variety of types of cricket with our friends in Enterprise. One was 'kneeling down' or 'marble' cricket. Our stumps were soft-drink bottles placed gingerly atop empty Carnation milk cans. We used soft stone or grass to draw a crease where we knelt on a beret, cap, piece of cardboard or wad of cloth while batting or bowling. A good wicket-keeper was extremely important in this game because after every attempted stroke a batsman had to 'ground' his bat. If he did not do this, he would almost certainly be stumped. Some lightning-fast keepers grew up amongst us. Sometimes merely shifting the bat outside the crease, or raising it a fraction from the ground led to the racket of bottles and cans being swept aside in one swift motion.

We played our miniature game with three kinds of ball. One was made simply by rolling a milk can until it was nearly round. Another was slightly more sophisticated. We took a stone and wrapped it in a piece of cloth. Snipping an inner tube from a bicycle tyre into tiny circular strands, we strapped these around the cloth until we had a ball. But the most preferred ball was the 'knit ball'. We soaked a quantity of paper, pressed and covered it with a piece of cloth, and then interlaced cord around the surface to form a solid, hard, durable object. Some of my friends were past masters at the art of knitting a ball. Individual styles abounded. Some lads would use a stone for the core, others tar from the streets. Some had their own designs and patterns for the surface. All of these objects had one feature in common: they were hard. My shins still carry the scars from playing at and missing one or other of these types of ball.

We also played a game called 'firms' or 'tip and run'. This was more like the traditional game of cricket in that you stood erect to bat and ran in to bowl. The main difference, from the usual game, was that you were forced to run if you struck the ball. It didn't matter where it went. The player who bowled a batsman or took a catch got a turn to bat. The game was called 'firms' presumably because any two players could co-operate. It was sensible for both members of the co-op to be batting at the same time; otherwise one could be run out simply by a member of another firm striking the ball directly to his partner. With an unlimited number of participants, one can easily imagine the confusion, noise, hilarity, and fun that was generated.

Unlike marble cricket, we had a wide range of balls to choose from for stand-up cricket. The most popular were large knit balls and tennis balls shaved of their fur. The bravest among us opted for the use of a 'compo' ball; a cork missile feared primarily because to be struck with it resulted in a bruised swelling. The compo ball is the hard nucleus of a normal cricket ball which we could sometimes get from an adult.

We made bats from the limbs of the 'clammy-cherry' or branches of the coconut tree. The 'clammy-cherry' was a little berry that exuded a sticky substance which formed the strongest bonding agent I can remember from my childhood. We used it to make kites, or to stick together any two or more paper objects we considered Nature to have mistakenly left unattached. The tree was also useful in providing the forked twigs for our catapults with which we stalked hapless ground doves and black birds, scaring them off more by our clumsiness than by our accuracy. We shaped bats from any suitable siding or other piece of board we could lay our hands on. Neighbours who owned palings or picket fences were well-advised to keep them in good repair for, at the slightest sign of damage, we descended on the offending carpentry like a band of marauders.

By the time I was eleven years old, my brother and I had helped our uncle to carve out an uneven, bumpy pitch behind our back yard. In the yard itself, all was industry and seriousness. Even the chickens, turkeys and ducks appeared to respect the need for order that Gran had firmly established. They never trespassed on each other's territory nor strayed into the other stock's confines. Beyond the galvanized fence, however, a world of freedom existed, symbolized by the strip of rolled dirt on which we played our cricket. The casuarina trees swayed in the gentle breeze that imitated the sound of the waves caressing the beach at the end of the lane. Only the lighthouse, firmly marking the cul-de-sac, gave any sign that there might be dangers lurking beyond our Eden.

When the others were unavailable for a game in the main road, Uncle Edwin would take us behind the paling for our cricket education. He knew that I could not play a leg break and that Bob could not bat at all. He would bat for long periods until one of us luckily got him out; then he would frustrate us by bowling our respective unplayable ball after we had made a couple of strokes, and we would be back in the hot sun plying away at him again.

Although we spent most of our recreational time playing cricket, Bob and I would also join Mosquito and Mullaback and the others in different activities. Enterprise is a mere eight miles from Bridgetown, the capital of Barbados, but because it is located in the cane belt, it is considered country and Bob and I country boys. Unlike most other areas in the cane belt, Enterprise is also on the coast. Our house was less than a mile from splendid beaches. Because of its location in the south of the island, the village had access to two different kinds of surf: the calm on the south western side for swimming, and the rough breakers from the Atlantic Ocean on the eastern side. Very early in life, boys learn to swim and soon put that skill to beneficial use when fishing in the choppy waters over the reefs.

We also used to go with the fishermen past the reefs to the open sea. Some of the older boys thought it funny to push the younger fellows off the boats and pretend to abandon them when they were barely within sight of land. Experiences like that forced me to become a reasonably good swimmer by the time I was twelve; but I never participated in aquatic sports, or considered swimming as a competitive exercise.

Once, when I was about seventeen, during an argument over some topic that I cannot now remember, Mullaback challenged me to an endurance contest. He said that he could force me to turn back in a swim out to sea. I knew Mulla's ability as a swimmer; but doubted that he could easily make me give up. We set off from the beach below the lighthouse, and after we had gone about a mile out to sea I realized that Mulla showed no intention of either tiring or returning to shore. I went along with him for another half mile before I accepted that common sense should come before pride. When I got back exhausted to the beach, the other boys ridiculed me for being a coward; but I suspected that the glow in their eyes also came from the respect they had for my courage in accepting the challenge and going so great a distance towards carrying it out.

Though swimming was not for medals, it was certainly for gain. As soon as I had learned how, I would equip myself with my home-made fish gun and mask and go off to the reefs to shoot fish. On many occasions, my catch supplemented Gran's vegetables for our dinner.

For the country boy with easy access to the sea, life was full: which meant in the language of the adults that the opportunities for mischief were legion. We played beach cricket; we ducked each other under the water and saw who could hold his breath the longest; we picked sea eggs from among the mussels; we organized races on the beach; and we went at night to pull crabs from their holes. In addition, we controlled what we considered unlimited acreage of sugar cane which was ours to plunder. In between the sugar cane fields, our private reserves of fruit and vegetables were being held in trust by planters who were under the impression that they were attempting to diversify their crops. Gran repeatedly told me during these years that I was never to steal and never to lie. When with the other boys I got round the practical inconvenience of obedience the way I imagined that the others did: I redefined the words. Stealing did not include taking pieces of sugar cane from a field and sucking the sweet, sticky juice until I couldn't move. Similarly, picking a papaya or a couple of apples was not stealing. I often painfully discovered that Gran held a completely different notion of theft. It also appeared that whatever activity provided the most fun became the one she hated most. Whenever I was caught in my attempts to re-interpret her commandments, Gran went through an amazing change. From the calm, concerned, reassuring lady who had, with a peck on the cheek, sent me out in the morning to play with the boys, she was transformed into a twig-wielding tyrant who seemed bent on separating my skin from my skeleton.

Cricket was the most common cause of the change that overcame Gran. Especially during the summer vacations, the boys in the village played cricket from sun-up until sun-down. I would be flogged for missing lunch. I would be flogged for forgetting to run an errand to the village shop when a cricket game had interrupted my progression towards my destination. I would be flogged for forgetting to tend the animals; and I imagined on those occasions that their bellowing and bleating were in exultation. As she brought the rod or strap down upon my back, the little lady with the terrific arm would always engage in the same kind of conversation. I knew that she was talking to herself, because on the rare occasions that I had tried to respond, she had made it clear that she expected no reply from me: 'I had this meal on the table for hours, and you refuse to eat it. Where do you think the money comes from? How can you afford to waste food?' It never dawned on her that if I had preferred food to cricket, I would have eaten instead of playing cricket. 'You told me that you would do this, Joel. You promised me. Joel, what are you becoming? What is to become of you?' Each word was accentuated by a stroke of the rod. Most often, the floggings were a result of the amount of time I spent playing cricket. 'Out all day in the hot sun? You ain't got anything else to do?'

Gran was small in stature; but she wielded a mean whip. I am surprised today that she was not more successful in her obvious intention to prevent me from playing the game at all. I think that after a while she got through to Bob. After a reasonably promising start he soon developed a strong dislike for cricket and an inability even to hold a bat properly. In my case, she failed. By the time I was twelve, my pals and I had begun to organize soft-ball games that were played in earnest among the villages within walking distance of Enterprise. We even had umpires who were required to be absolutely unbiased.

Normally, the soft-ball games would be played on any open patch of ground in the neighbourhood. The group of youngsters from that area would have spent a considerable amount of time during the week looking for a suitable 'wicket', watering the dirt strip, and rolling it until it was hard and smooth. They would acquire dry donkey or cow manure, break it into pieces and roll it into the dirt. We thought that the flat surface that resulted closely resembled the test wicket at Kensington.

If there were no large open spaces in a particular neighbourhood we would simply set up stumps at any location which provided a little open space. In all seriousness the two captains would meet and decide vitally important issues: 'Past the old car down there is four. In the air is six. The ackee tree yonder is the boundary. No, first hop is not an out.' A disgruntled old person always seemed to live within striking distance of our matches. We often found that we had established our wicket near the house of someone who did not appreciate having their wooden house constantly bombarded on Saturday mornings. And they didn't take kindly to the noisy banter of the players and spectators at our games. Once we identified where the person lived, we made a rule: hitting that house is an out. They were always the same people; you avoided, at all costs, hitting the ball into their back yards for, if by chance the ball landed there, no hope existed of getting it back. Many a close-fought game met a premature end through such an accident. Today, I can understand the discomfort we caused our neighbours, many of whom depended upon their back-yard gardens for extra cash and survival and who were unwilling to allow their handiwork to be destroyed by young rascals. At the time, I often wondered whether God had not put a select group of people on earth whose sole function was to make a boy's life miserable.

These people did not prevent perfect childhood happiness only on weekends. During the week, they changed their clothes and became teachers. Although school was a very important part of the Barbadian country boy's life, just as the island is a tropical paradise in which sunshine is intermittently interrupted by rain, so, in the midst of an ideal childhood, the thunderstorm of school prevented the continuous enjoyment we all sought.

My first school was St Christopher's Boys. The building was an Anglican church where services were held on Sundays and discipline imposed during the week. I ran into a quiet lad called Randolph on my very first day at school and he is to this day a very close friend on whom I can depend. His friendship helped me through the trials of school. He made life at St Christopher's relaxed. In truth he was as troublesome as any of the other children, but you wouldn't have been able to get any of the teachers to believe that. He used his naturally angelic features to deceive teachers into believing that he could do no wrong. Many an innocent lad has been punished in his stead. As his friend, some of the favouritism he received flowed my way. Mr Lynch, the headmaster, tried his best to make the school experience enjoyable for the boys. We had our milk and biscuit breaks and classes were held outside the building under the trees that surrounded it. Randolph and I used to be amused when we could see one of the boys from another class being flogged, but we had to exercise great care not to be caught laughing either by our teacher or the victim.

The teachers were strict and every once in a while the entire class would feel their wrath; but 'Milto' Millington and 'Big Drop' Clarke were for the most part patient and kind people, even though they refused us the pleasure of using their nicknames to their faces. I don't think that we would have dared in any case because of our fear and respect for them.

After the eleven-plus examinations, I left St Christopher's and attended secondary school at Foundation Boys. I was sorry to leave the old primary school behind. Cricket had begun to tighten its grip on me by this time. I had continued playing in the village competitions and behind our yard. I had also continued to watch my uncle's team which played on the wicket further down the casuarina-lined lane that led to the lighthouse. I was delighted when I got the opportunity to field in the odd game when one of the players had not turned up on time. Although I was proud to do this and thoroughly enjoyed myself, I sometimes ran into trouble. I remember during one game when I had a simple catch come to me and I dropped it. I could not control myself at having let slip such an easy chance and I laughed. The captain was angry beyond words; and sent me off the field with motions of his arms and without uttering a sound. League players took their cricket seriously: there was no place for a laughing kid.

I did reasonably well as a student at Foundation, and the teachers had little trouble disciplining me because by then the values Gran had instilled at home had become second nature.

I did my work to the best of my ability, stayed away from the more delinquent boys, and did my homework under Gran's watchful eye. But most of all, I played cricket. I had quickly found that it was cricket of a different kind to the type I had played at Enterprise. The school provided equipment and coaching. I discovered that whilst wearing pads it was unnecessary to shy away from the fast bowlers. You can imagine my astonishment the first time I played at a ball and missed. The ball struck my shins; but the pain to which I had become accustomed was absent. The pads protected my legs. 'Oh, yeah,' I thought, 'this is going to be easy.' In the school's set matches and in net practice I prided myself on being a batsman.

In my twelfth year I was still a stripling of a lad. Much to the surprise of those who have only met me since my school days, I was no taller than the others in the first form at Foundation; and by no means the tallest in the class. If I had been, I might have avoided a couple of painful experiences. Once, during that year, we were about to have our English lesson and study the *Rhyme of the Ancient Mariner*. Mr Prescod, our English master, was a tall, severe man who exerted pressure and punishment on his charges out of all proportion to their willingness to learn. I had been made the class monitor, which meant that I was left in charge of the other boys when no master was around.

On the day in question, the boys were banging their desktops and creating a horrible amount of noise. They were beyond my control and I was looking forward to Mr Prescod's arrival. One boy was stationed at the door as a lookout and he suddenly rushed back to his seat. The noise stopped abruptly. When Mr Prescod entered the room, he was met by a group of the most innocent-looking faces one could imagine.

'Good morning,' he said to the class.

'Good morning, sir,' we answered.

'Joel, was this the class from which I heard that noise on my way up the corridor?' he asked.

Before I knew what was happening my mouth had opened and I heard the words coming out as if from some other place. 'Yes, sir,' I said.

'All of you will stay in after class this afternoon and write 200 times the first verse of the poem you should have been reading instead of creating such a racket.'

A collective groan came from the students. I glanced around to find that most of them were staring at me threateningly. I felt like the bird we were reading about. For the duration of the lesson I concentrated hard on what we were supposed to be doing, although I can't say that I could see a single word on the page.

At the break afterwards, all the others filed out of the room. I felt ashamed for squealing on them and sat at my desk alone and dejected. After a while, my friend Derek, who had been one of the ring-leaders and who had banged his desk the loudest, poked his head around the door and said with a smile, 'Joel, come here a minute.'

When I got outside the classroom, I found that the boys had formed a gauntlet along the two sides of the corridor and I was made to run along it with my hands up to protect my head and eyes while they each tore into me with the belts they had taken from their trousers.

That was to be my last experience of that kind. Threats of various kinds have been made against me since then, but I have never had occasion to be involved in a fight. During the summer before my thirteenth birthday, I grew remarkably fast. I shot into the air almost overnight. I don't know what caused it. Gran was an excellent cook and like all Barbadian cooks she was heavy on starch, carbohydrates and quantity; but she hadn't cooked any differently that summer. All I know is that I left the classroom in June a stripling of average height, and returned that September a full head taller than most of the others in the school, including many of the teachers. I never again had to demand respect.

Under constant coaching from Gran and Uncle Edwin, my academic performance was kept up to scratch. Most of my schoolmates looked forward to becoming clerks in the Civil Service or in one of the local banks. To achieve a white collar job was to have 'made it'. I harboured a desire to become a policeman which was reinforced by Gran in the background always insisting that I be successful at what I tried. 'Make something of yourself, boy. Get a good education. They can take everything away from you; but they can't take away what you've got in your head.' I didn't know at that time whom she meant by 'they', and I couldn't understand how or why 'they' would want to take anything away from me.

What I was doing, while maintaining an average academic standard for her satisfaction, was playing cricket. In Barbados at the time there were four levels of officially-played cricket. At the top there were the Division One teams of the Barbados Cricket Association. This consisted of the players who had either made or would like to make the Barbados and West Indies teams. Some of the schools had First Division teams, so it was possible for schoolboys to play against the very best players on the island. The second tier of official cricket was the Intermediate Division from which players hoped to be promoted to a First Division side, and the third level was the Second Division.

The BCA divisions formed a class above the fourth level of cricket that was most popular among the villagers in Enterprise. The cricket they enjoyed was hard, but the level of performance and achievement rivalled anything offered in the First Division. This was the Barbados Cricket League game; it was played among the local clubs and was a natural development out of the self-organized village games on local grounds.

The class structure of Barbadian society was almost perfectly reflected in the structure of its cricket. There were no 'upper class gents' playing BCL cricket. Those were to be found in teams like Wanderers, Pickwick or Carlton. On the other hand, the BCL teams were most often named after the villages or areas they represented. When two of these teams met, they were defending home turf. It was a question of territorial rights. The wickets were prepared to suit the particular strengths of the home side; and other rewards apart from winning a game of cricket were at stake. The stakes had something to do with prestige, and in certain cases an element that had something to do with manhood and the struggle to survive also existed. At that time some of the most competitive and heated cricket in Barbados was played in the BCL. If a BCL player ever got the chance to play against a team from the BCA, or even against individual BCA players (and they rarely got this opportunity apart from net practice or the odd event in which the BCL player was so outstanding that he was called to trials for the Barbados team) what resulted was nothing short of war. I grew up with tales of BCL fast bowlers who were demon pacers: aggressive, hostile, apparently hating each and every batsman confronting them. They were bowlers like Charlie Griffith, 'Hitler' Downes and 'Grey Patch' Mascoll who gained a great deal of pleasure from hitting batsmen. I had heard stories of how these bowlers, confronted in the nets by a 'class' batsman would have to be prevented from bowling because of the danger to the batsman.

In my area, we had BCL teams like Thornbury Hill, Warwickshire, Sherewood, Scarborough, Walls, Kent, Searle's' Boys' Club, and our local side Southpoint for which Uncle Edwin played. Southpoint had outstanding batsmen like Pudgy, Scarlett, Neville Bradshaw, Manny, Kermitt, and the two King brothers, one of whom was also a gifted leg-break bowler. These men could hit a ball harder than anyone else I have ever seen. They were accomplished players who could read a game and put into effect what was necessary to bring about a predicted outcome. We also had really fast bowlers in Jack Hobbs, Martin Williams and Harlon Sealy. My uncle and Kari Agard were also good medium-fast bowlers.

Every Saturday, after we had played our own village games, the youngsters would watch these matches and witness performances that went beyond the ordinary struggles of a cricket game. A good batsman in the BCL was a batsman of exceptional talent. Uncoached, untutored in any way other than through raw experience and watching others, they possessed skills that test players might envy. When the local team played against Sherewood, another Christ Church team, to the local people it was the equivalent of watching a Shell Shield game. Hundreds of spectators turned up for these matches.

The special preparation of the wickets was part and parcel of the home team's effort. As we grew older, Mosquito and I were responsible for preparing the wickets, and we always made them suitable for our fast bowlers. We used detergent and sea water, and the wicket at Southpoint was always fast and slippery. Other sides dreaded playing us at home, unless they had comparable fast bowlers of their own.

Whilst still at school, I joined with the other lads to form a cricket team we called Winchester, a name not supposed to refer to the cathedral but to the rifle. Some of the fellows that we played against also played BCL cricket. There was a rule that schoolboys should not play BCL cricket, but some of the better players did so and got away with it. Their allegiance to their respective villages was greater than their loyalty to school. On the whole, if you were good enough to represent the school, even at Second Division cricket, you would choose to do this rather than play BCL cricket because the chances of making it into a First Division side were better.

When I was fourteen years old, I played Second Division cricket for Foundation School as an all-rounder. Almost immediately I moved up into the Intermediate side. At the time, we were coached by Seymour Nurse, the ex-West Indies batsman, for whom all the boys had a great deal of respect. We all considered him one of the very best batsmen Barbados had produced. Seymour Nurse's batting had a feature that all Bajans enjoy and appreciate: flair. He was good not only at piling up runs, but he did so apparently effortlessly and gracefully. The Bajan cricket-watching public would never allow Geoff Boycott the same acclaim they reserve for Gary Sobers or Tom Graveney, no matter how many runs Boycott might make. The style of making the runs for us is as important as the number of runs made. Chimp Lashley, Mullaback, and Mosquito have all left Kensington Oval after having watched Sobers make twenty or Lawrence Rowe only a few. They felt fully satisfied that they had watched batting at its best. Seymour Nurse was in that company as far as we were concerned. We were grateful, and considered ourselves fortunate that he was our coach.

I was particularly happy that Nurse was our coach, because, although I had made a few runs for the school's second eleven side, not even Gran would have considered my batting graceful, though from time to time I had made some strokes that would match the smoothest of them. I thought that Nurse could show me how to develop that slow, nonchalant stroke play. Instead, he gave me the shock of my life.

During the second or third session that we had with Seymour Nurse at Foundation, I was batting and really enjoying it. I also thought that I looked particularly good when Nurse shouted to me from where he was standing behind the nets. 'Garner,' he said, 'What's a big fellow like you doing batting or trying to bat? You're much too big to be a batsman.' I was shocked. He must have noticed the bewildered look on my face.

'With your height, son, you should be bowling, fast.' He placed such an emphasis on the word 'fast' that his meaning was clear.

He drew me aside and lectured me on how to take full advantage of my height. He insisted that I should in no way compromise this natural advantage by bending my back or lowering my arm at the moment of delivery, but instead should use it to the fullest. He said that if I used my height properly, my chances of success in cricket as a bowler would be better.

I cannot clearly remember now, but he must have been most diplomatic in relaying this information to me at a time when I considered myself one of the better batsmen in the school team. I only bowled if I could not avoid it. In Barbados, cricket is a batsman's game. Not many boys grow up wanting to be a fast bowler. They are the drudges of the game. We bowled because it was through bowling that we got a chance to bat. But I am forever grateful to Seymour Nurse for recognizing whatever potential I might have had, and for having the judgement and common sense to put it across to me in a way that would be acceptable.

So I began to bowl as quickly as I could with a double-pump action that I thought not only pretty, but a great help to the inswinger that came naturally. Then, in addition to the coaching clinics at school, I began to attend the coaching sessions that Charlie Griffith and Gary Sobers were organizing at the BCL headquarters.

Charlie, an old BCL player before joining the First Division team Empire, was an enthusiastic teacher. He appeared to have a driving desire to give young bowlers that aggressiveness and will to win that I felt, even at the time, was an attempt to pass on his legacy to another generation of Barbadian fast bowlers. With Charlie, cricket ceased to be fun. Like everything else that he did, the coaching sessions were essays in seriousness and application. Above all, during those sessions, Charlie gave me a feeling of pride in being a fast bowler. Renowned for a devastating yorker, he taught me how to bowl one that swung in the air. He also showed how a bouncer could be used effectively, not only to intimidate the batsman but also as part of a wider strategy for getting him out. And, most important, he stopped me from using the double-swing action with which I had always bowled. He pointed out that it reduced rhythm and fluency while preventing the natural development of the delivery from run-up through release. The result was a reduction in the speed of the ball. Later, watching Max Walker of Australia, I saw just how right Charlie was.

With all that I had learned, I thought that getting into the school's second eleven side would be easy. As in all organizations involving schoolboys, the side was run by a clique. The captain had the final word in choosing members to play on Saturdays. I grew to suspect that his friends got picked whatever their abilities or form. There was a nucleus of five or six players that would play every week. And this nucleus was made up of boys from the Scarborough and Church Hill areas who were always saying that I was not good enough to play with them. Although I wanted to play cricket regularly and considered it an honour to play for the school, I really did not want to play in a side that I felt was unfairly chosen. I continued to play on Saturdays for Winchester and to watch BCL cricket while the school team played its matches. But I also continued to go to net practices at school.

One Friday afternoon at practice, someone said that one of the regulars on the Ronald Tree side was ill and there would be a place for another player. The captain approached me and asked me if I would play. I forgot my qualms about the composition of the side and agreed to play. During the game against another school team from Coleridge and Parry, I batted at number eleven and top-scored in both innings. In another game against Lodge, I took seven wickets after the opposition had appeared not in the least worried by the attack of the first four bowlers. Imagine my surprise the following Saturday when I overheard other members of the team muttering that I should not be allowed to get eight or nine wickets. I was not given the ball for the remainder of the game. I was angry and vowed never again to play Second Division cricket for Foundation.

As it turned out, my anger was wasted, because some members of the school's Intermediate team had seen part of my performance and I was invited to move up into that division where selection was made more on merit than on friendship.

During my last year at school, I played Intermediate cricket and sat my GCE O level examinations. I also got called for trials for the youth team, and represented the Barbados team against the Combined Islands at the Carlton grounds. A stroke of good fortune allowed me to play in the team at that time because, had I not been born in December, then I would have been too old. I remember the game well for an experience that had little to do with cricket. A group of the lads with whom I had grown up went with me to the ground. They shared the pride of my achievement in being selected; and it was a happy bunch of us that converged on Carlton that morning. It was one of my last experiences as a schoolboy, and one of the most moving.

3

Unknown to me at the time, Wes Hall, that great and elegant fast bowler who, together with Charlie Griffith, struck fear in the hearts of international batsmen during the sixties, had watched me closely in an Intermediate game that Foundation School had played against Cable and Wireless. Wes was the personnel officer with that company and played for their cricket team on weekends. Much later, he told me that he had assured other members of his side that I would one day play for Barbados and the West Indies.

Such ideas were not in my head then. I had done my school-leaving examinations and was awaiting the results. Like the rest of my school-mates, I was then standing on the edge of the chasm between youth and manhood. I therefore set out to find a job, attempting to follow Gran's advice to 'get a good one. One with a future.' I got the necessary forms to apply to join the police force, but put them aside while I waited for my results. In the meantime, I came across an advertisement for vacancies at Cable and Wireless and sent off an application. I really didn't expect too much to come of it, and I was surprised when I was called for an interview.

Although I hadn't yet got my examination results, I was accepted to study at the company's training school to become a telegraph operator. To this day, I don't know if Wes Hall had anything to do with my appointment at Cable and Wireless, although from time to time I have suspected that he did. I was happy to join the company because among its ranks were some of the best cricketers at the Intermediate level on the island. It was unusual to find fewer than four ex-test players in the clubhouse on a Saturday. In addition, the job held the kind of prestige in Barbados that would make Gran happy.

David Husbands was another one of the people who kept a

close watch on my career. I just came into contact with him as a youngster walking home from school, he would give my brother and I a lift home. At the time of the meeting he was seeing one of the girls in my district whom he later married. Subsequently he has kept all my statistics on every game. He has lived in the area since then and we have become very good friends. An off-break bowler and gully fielder, he has even played intermediate cricket for Cable and Wireless with me.

I found the work at Cable and Wireless easy, and the staff friendly. The men with whom I worked were only too willing to help. I don't think that I would have made it without them. Sam Eastmond, for example, was then one of the supervisors at the office, and if I had a problem of a game of cricket clashing with the times that I should be on duty, he would always find a way to allow me to change shifts. It is not only for this reason that I consider him a true friend, confidant and adviser. He was later to play a vitally important role in my decision to play cricket in the Lancashire League. Sparkie Cummings and Michael Seale were among the staff members who would exchange their duties with mine so that I could play cricket, even when it caused them personal inconvenience. If I noticed that the duty roster had me down to work on a day when I had to play cricket, I could depend on one of the lads to take over for me while I slipped off. Even after I had left Cable and Wireless' team, the guys in the operating room continued to stand in for me when I needed to be elsewhere.

I had a lot of help on the cricket field as well. Wes Hall had by then retired from first-class cricket, but continued to play Intermediate for Cable and Wireless as the team's captain and fast bowler. During my first year there, Wes began to keep wicket, a position he once held as a schoolboy and one whose arts he still thinks he masters. He did this primarily to coach me as a fast bowler. His advice was invaluable. Many of my wickets during a highly successful season resulted from his suggestions. During my second year at Cable, Wes came from behind the stumps and opened the bowling with me. One of the aspects of the craft that he especially tried to drum into my head was how to use the crease. At that time, I would simply run up as fast as I could and let fly. He taught me the effectiveness of bowling outswingers from wide of the crease.

We had arguments about the crease when I would say that I didn't see the sense of the bowler taking too much notice of the crease apart from trying not to bowl a no-ball. Wes would say, 'Man, utilize the crease. There's going to come a time when you'll be bowling from the same spot and nothing is going to happen. You're going to have to rub the ball a bit more, pull at your collar, anything to throw the batsman off. The crease is more useful than the rest of these antics.'

I used to say that if I could move the ball both ways I didn't see why I should be too concerned about that. Later, when it did turn out that I would bowl for a long time from the same spot, doing the same things with the ball, with the batsman playing me with the dead centre of the bat, I found that by bowling that bit wider, the angle became slightly different and I could distract the batsman more.

At around this time, I was in the process of developing one of the greatest obstacles to any type of success: a big ego. At first I argued about much of the advice Wes offered. Things were not the same as when he had been a wicket-keeper. Now he was bowling with me and in some ways I considered him a competitor. We used to have the most heated discussions about aspects of my bowling that he sought to change. Fortunately for me, my head never got so big that I would not at least try some of the things he suggested.

Wes was invariably correct in the advice he offered, which did much for the development of whatever talent I have. He was particularly good at explaining the difference between delivery points: where the ball is actually released, and the resulting variation in pace and length. He also taught me the importance of direction and how to bowl accurately. He could be as detailed as a coaching manual in emphasizing the importance of rhythm and approach to the crease and in explaining that the bowler's head should be held absolutely still at the moment of delivery. Thanks to him, I came to regard fast bowling as a craft. Before playing with him I had thought that natural talent was mostly responsible for getting batsmen out. He taught me that this is far from being the case; he also tried to teach me how to listen.

I remember an episode after I had left Cable and Wireless' team and was playing for YMPC in the First Division. We were playing against the local brewery team at the Banks ground, and the home side was a strong one. My bowling partner was a quickie called Gumbs. George Brathwaite, one of the more experienced of the Banks players, had come in to open the innings. After about eight overs, not a single short-pitched delivery had been bowled because Gumbs had cautioned me not to bowl short at this man. I couldn't understand why I shouldn't bowl short at Brathwaite who looked as if he would have been more at home cutting grass than facing fast bowlers. He hardly looked the type to be nimble enough to fend off a good bouncer, and in fact I interpreted Gumbs' suggestion as a veiled attempt to protect him. After a couple of half volleys that Brathwaite stroked sweetly through the covers, I decided to ignore Gumbs' advice and let fly with a bouncer. I watched in utter amazement as for one moment the ball looked as if it would decapitate the man and the next instant it was flying over the fence at backward square leg and heading for the adjoining residential district.

I thought that Brathwaite's shot was a lucky one, and proceeded to bowl a second bouncer, this time faster than the first. It too disappeared towards the same spot as the previous ball, only this time it went a little farther. I didn't bowl short at Brathwaite again. I didn't ignore Gumbs' advice again, either. I will never forget the smiles that he and Brathwaite wore for the rest of the game.

Whilst playing for Cable and Wireless, I began to gain something of a reputation. My confidence in my ability also grew. In one knock-out game against a strong Police team, Cable and Wireless were only able to give the opposition 56 runs to win. As we were taking the field, I overheard the Police opening batsmen joking that they could knock off the runs in a hurry. I told the other players on my side that we would have to play this game as if it were a war. The opposition's fans laughed loudly then, but were not laughing an hour and a half later when, thanks only to a sitter being dropped, they barely won by one wicket.

I twice went to trials for the Barbados team, and on both occasions failed to gain a place in the side. I thought that I was performing well. I had figures that were among the best, and could not understand why I was constantly overlooked. It was no consolation to discuss matters with Hugh Gore, a Barbadian who captained the Combined Islands youth team, and Nigel Johnson, who, during the 1972 youth tournament was the most outstanding batsman with three centuries in four games and a record aggregate.

Neither of these truly talented players was to play consistently for their national team, and Johnson was to make it into the Barbados side only when he was much older and had doubtless lost much of his youthful zest. They both thought that social class in the West Indies played as great a part in the selection process as ability. I myself began to draw similar conclusions from some of the experiences I could remember from my school days. The mysterious 'they' that Gran had spoken about began to take definite shape; and although I began to grow increasingly angry at 'them' I tried to contain this anger and made up my mind that I would break through their barriers by serious application to my game.

One day, disappointed after having been refused selection to the Barbados team yet again, I ran into Peter Lashley in the office cafeteria. Peter had been a useful left-handed batsman for Barbados and the West Indies. He worked at Cable and Wireless and played cricket for Spartan club in Division One. He was a shrewd reader of the game both on and off the field. On this occasion, Peter doubtless knew why I appeared depressed. He drew me aside and said simply, 'Bird, you'll never play cricket for Barbados from an Intermediate team.'

Peter is not one to waste words. He is respected as an astute person by all who know him. I also felt that he held no malice towards me and was genuinely trying to help; but I knew that there had been at least a couple of players who had done precisely what he was now suggesting was impossible.

'Is that so, Peter?' I asked. 'Then how do you account for Vannie Holder and Michael Walcott?'

Peter was characteristically unmoved. 'Bird,' he said, 'you don't understand what I mean. I said that *you* will never play for Barbados from an Intermediate team.'

The force of what he said and how he had said it struck me as if I had been punched.

Peter's remark remained with me for a couple of weeks during which time I consulted all those who had given me advice about such things before. I understood that, in the last resort, it was left up to me to make a decision. I got a number of conflicting suggestions. There were those who thought that I certainly had the ability to play for Barbados and that all that was required was patience until the selectors came to see that I should be afforded an opportunity. Others agreed with Peter's idea that to play for Barbados, one needed to be a member of a First Division club. They thought that it would be unfair to overlook the players who faced tougher opponents and give a chance to a bowler performing well against second-class opposition. There were also those who thought that I would never make the side whether I performed well at Intermediate or First Division level. These people would never spell out the reasons for their convictions but left the issue to be read from between the lines: I was from the wrong side of the tracks. My own answer to this could only be to keep performing at as high a level as I could maintain.

I came to agree with the logic of what Peter had said. It appeared to me that I had no option. I had been invited to a couple of trials for the Barbados team; but had failed to make the side although in my own estimation I was at least as good as some of the other bowlers with whom I competed for a place and who finally made it. There had to be a reason, and I found Peter's the most palatable. I had even begun to ask myself if I would ever realize my ambition of playing for Barbados. I would spend hours when I was swimming alone or sitting around with friends, asking myself what the possible reasons could be for my inability to make the team. I had even begun to feel that someone up there in the hierarchy of the Barbados Cricket Association did not like me.

The short chat with Peter Lashley was only one of a number of occasions from which I grew to learn more and more about the character of Barbados cricket and the social influences that affected the game. After I had finally secured a place in the Barbados side, I once went to sit in the stands with Mosquito, Saga and Chimp. It was the luncheon interval, and I just wanted to chat with them a while before play restarted. Because of force of circumstances, my friends were not among the best-dressed gentlemen watching the cricket. To those who do not know them, they probably appear a bunch of juvenile delinquents. I know them to be honest, forthright, generous and concerned. After I had chatted with them for a while and put up with their ribbing and jokes, and was on my way back to the players' dressing room, I ran into one of the stalwarts of the Barbados Cricket Association who, without breaking straight-backed stride or even looking in my direction, muttered in a scolding tone, 'If you want to play this cricket, you will have to watch the kind of friends you keep.'

More fortunate for my chances of representing the West Indies was the fact that he was gone before I could take the opportunity to give him what I still consider would have been an appropriate response.

Finally, after conversations with Hugh Gore, Michael Walcott and Collis King, I decided to leave Cable and Wireless' team and join a First Division side. My choices were limited. Wanderers, Pickwick, and Carlton, though all changing to accept a few Black players who suited them, were predominantly and traditionally white clubs. I thought that even if I wanted to play for one of these sides I could not suffer the indignity of having my application for membership refused. I didn't want to have to face that. Spartan was a team of Black players; but they were Black middle-class players and I didn't want to have to put up with that either. I had practised at Empire, another Black club in Division One, and had been a schoolboy member, but I did not like what I saw there in terms of the team spirit. It seemed to me that the side was made up of eleven prima donnas, and I could not imagine how I could function among them.

Primarily because of Collis King's advice, I eventually made up my mind to join YMPC where Collis played. The players on this team had the same kinds of backgrounds as mine. To be honest, also, I could not resist the temptation of becoming a big fish in a little pond. YMPC at the time was one of the weaker sides in the BCA First Division.

I was not happy to leave the Cable team. In addition to the friendships that I had made through playing with fellow workers, my bowling had improved since leaving school. I took 95 wickets from 11 matches in the last year that I played with them and was one of five cricketers of the year.

When I joined YMPC, I was immediately made to feel at home. My friendship with Collis King grew very close. This was a man who played hard at everything he did. A cricket lover who has not seen Collis bat has missed a great treat. He struck the ball extremely hard, was not very pretty to watch but was extremely effective. Off the field, he was always ready to provide advice and help.

The person whom I met at YMPC and who was to have the most influence on my future was Duncan Carter, a pace bowler of wide experience who had played in both the Central and Lancashire Leagues in England. After my first year at YMPC, and after I had finally succeeded in making the Barbados team for a couple of Shell Shield games against the Islands and Jamaica, he asked me if I would like to play professional cricket in England. I told him that I would have to think about it.

I had no idea what playing professional cricket was all about. I had bowled well in the two chances I had finally been given to represent Barbados, including 3 for 18 from 10 overs against the Combined Islands, only to find myself as thirteenth man in the squad chosen against the Jamaican side in 1976. I was disappointed. It appeared to me that I would play for Barbados only when the first string players were overseas; as had happened in the Shell tournament when Vanburn Holder and Keith Boyce were in Australia playing for the West Indies. I thought that I had little future in Barbadian cricket and, at the same time, I had become bored with my job as an operator with Cable and Wireless.

At a crucial moment when time was running out before I had to answer Duncan Carter concerning the contract to replace Gary Sobers at Littleborough in the Central Lancashire League, I approached my supervisor at Cable and Wireless and sought his advice. Sam Eastmond was to the point. 'Do you want to play cricket?' he asked.

'Of course I do,' I answered.

'Then take up the contract in the League,' he said.

'What about the job?' I demanded. I felt that he was taking my situation too lightly. I still had to support Gran.

'Bird,' Sam said, 'let me tell you something about Barbados that you don't seem to know. You could bowl your ass off for YMPC every Saturday and get the most wickets in the BCA and

be the most promising youngster and all that. And still one of
the professionals would come from the Leagues or the Counties
and walk into the team and you would be left on the outside.
Barbados respects achievement overseas more than it does
brilliance at home. Besides, there's only a couple of years
difference between promising youngster and old has-been.'
    I decided to accept Duncan's offer.

Duncan Carter arranged every aspect of my trip to England.
He even got the airplane tickets for me. I knew nothing about
contracts or about England beyond what I had read in books,
and Duncan never broke my trust. Because of him and his hard
work, especially his ability to deal with Gran, who was doubtful
about the whole idea of flying off to a distant land merely to
play a silly game, I found myself on a flight out of Barbados
in April 1976 headed for what Bajans normally call 'over in
away'.
    I flew from Barbados to England on 16 April 1976 with Collis
King. On arrival I was taken to Leyton in London to spend the
day with some friends, Richard and Cheryl, who had emigrated
to join their mother and stepfather, Jean and Bert Thornhill,
and their youngest sister, Helen, who was born in the UK. Little
did I know then that they would become my adopted family in
Britain. Ever since that first meeting I have been accepted as
though I was one of their own, being given keys to the house
and a bed. Over the years the bond has become very close. We
are always in touch and I have the greatest respect for the
family and their sincerity. Perhaps words are inadequate to
express my heartfelt thanks and gratitude.
    During my first year in the UK I lived at Duncan's house
with his family. The ex-policeman is an extremely quiet man
and another of the many Barbadians who have been willing to
give me only the best advice. I think that while living in
Swinton, about eleven miles from Manchester, I learnt more
than enough about the English way of life. I found it extremely
strange that you could say 'good morning' to someone and be
greeted with a look of surprise that you actually spoke. In
Barbados, it is considered rude on meeting someone, even a
total stranger, not to greet them.
    Living in an area where we were the only Black family was

also strange. Unlike Barbados, there was no one on the street to turn to for friendship. When I took a walk, dozens of eyes turned in my direction, and at first I tried hard to figure out whether it was because of my height or for some other reason. I felt totally out of my element. Duncan more than once drew me aside and told me just to be polite, keep myself to myself, and not to bother about anything until I grew to understand what was going on. He looked after me as though I was his son. Pauline, his wife, who chatted far more than he ever did, was also very helpful and made sure that I was always comfortable. She reminded me so much of my Gran that in a short while I didn't really miss home apart from the beach and the boys in the gap. But because of the absence of any real friends, I spent most of the days when I was not playing cricket watching TV with Duncan and his daughter Hazel.

Slowly I became accustomed to the pace of things. I met an Australian, John Garritty, who had at first only come over to England on holiday and later decided that he wanted a season in the Leagues. He was a competent wicket-keeper who later told me that he played seconds at Dennis Lillee's club in Australia. I spent a great deal of time with him. I guess that he thought himself as much of an outsider as I was because the older club members at Littleborough were constantly complaining about his lifestyle and his hippie-length hair. I also met the Bamfords who owned a pub in Heywood. I used to go out drinking with Mick when I was not hanging around his pub. Old man Doug, and Peter, his son, were also quite close. They would lend me their car to get around the area, and even after I left and began playing for Somerset they would take me to games. So, after a while I had made a few friends and found that life in England could be much like that in Barbados, apart of course from the beaches and the food.

On the other hand, I met a man, Roger Lord, who I think was victimized and ostracized by some of his friends because of me. We used to travel to a lot of games together and afterwards stop off for the regular pint of Lager and Sam. He often ran into trouble with his girlfriends because of his hanging around with me and I think that I cost him quite a few.

Fred Harmer, the chairman of the club, and his wife Ethel also took a liking to me. They are two of the nicest people one would ever want to meet, anywhere. For a while, I lived in their son's house while he was away at work. Jack Hunter, too, tried to make the change from the Caribbean to English conditions as smooth as possible. I learnt a lot from him about the inconsistencies of English life. Although one of the oldest members of the team, he was an extremely good player and very young at heart. He was the centre of attraction for the team.

When I got particularly homesick, in spite of the efforts of my English friends, I would frequent the West Indian Social Clubs where I came into contact with some of the home-folk like the Blades brothers; Roy Gilchrist, once without doubt the fastest bowler in the world and the most dangerous if riled; Ces Wright, Douggie Clarke and Roy Browne. Roy used to lend me his car, and always took me along on the family excursions to different English cities and to Scotland, which I thoroughly enjoyed.

With a solid group of friends around to protect me from the more uncomfortable aspects of life in England, plus the activities on the cricket field, that first year in England passed quickly. I was told that the summer of 1976 was one of record temperatures in England, but that suited me fine. It still felt extremely cold in the mornings and sometimes after the day's play was done. I was impressed by the beauty of the English countryside with its intense greens, especially in the mornings when invariably a light mist would settle over the ground and give the landscape the appearance of some classical painting.

I managed to bowl well for Littleborough that year. Duncan Carter gave me a lot of advice about how to bowl in the Leagues where the wickets differed from ground to ground. Les Fisk, our groundsman, used to ask me what kind of wicket the opposition had prepared every time we played an away game. If I told him that it was a marl one, which was too often the case, he would respond in the same way every time. 'Don't worry, son. Wait 'til they get here.'

I got 110 wickets and made 507 runs, and Littleborough won the Wood Cup and came fourth in the championship after a start in which all the players felt that we would win. The Littleborough supporters began to call me 'Little Bird' which was refreshing after some of the things I was called on some of the other grounds. At times, I didn't think that those loudmouths really liked the batsmen on the team they were supposed to be supporting. It is difficult not to take it out on an opposing batsman when someone on the boundary calls out to you that you should get back to the jungle or shouts some insulting name. I honestly feel that the supporters were responsible for the number of batsmen injured during that season.

What made that first season most enjoyable though was that Duncan, in spite of injury that forced him to miss many games, finished with 63 wickets and 630 runs. It was a very happy Bird that bade goodbye to the Carters at the end of the season and flew back to Barbados and Enterprise, and the beach. I hoped that the Barbadian selectors read the English newspapers. In any case, in my pocket I had a contract to play for Littleborough the following year. Lady Luck was on my side.

4

Let me say from the outset that even while some commentators were calling the cricket matches organized by Kerry Packer a circus, I considered the move nothing less than a phase in the structural development of West Indian cricket. I would not have joined the group of West Indian cricketers who signed up to play under Mr Packer's auspices had I not felt that it was the right thing to do. My reasons for joining were, of course, primarily financial; but there were other considerations as well.

By the time that I had been chosen to represent the West Indies against Pakistan in 1977, I saw my selection as the end of a process that had taken a long time. For almost all of my life I had thought about playing cricket for the West Indies; but I was also aware that I would have to get a steady job in case I didn't make it, and, perhaps even if I did. For my first test match against Pakistan, my salary was very poor. I never expected to become rich overnight from playing cricket; but compared to other sportsmen, cricketers were extremely poorly paid for their talents. It was clear that I could not continue to rely solely upon cricket for a livelihood if this was going to be the money I would be paid. In the West Indies, jobs have, from time to time, been given to ex-test players in the form of government coaching appointments. There are also innumerable cases of ex-test players who face old age without a pension after their years of toiling. Unless the West Indian test player used great care in managing his finances, he had to face a pretty uncertain future.

After my first year in the Central Lancashire League, I had been approached by a representative of Somerset County Cricket Club to play in England in the summer of 1977; but I had little to look forward to by way of a secure future in West

Indies cricket. You only got paid when you played. It had taken six years for me to reach the top. When I was finally chosen to represent the West Indies a couple of times, I wanted to make sure that I would keep my place in the team; but I had also given up my job as a telegraph operator to play in the Leagues. I was supporting my grandmother, and I wanted her whom I loved dearly to have the basic comforts in her old age. It was the least that I could do for Gran after all that she had done for me. You might say that I was vulnerable to 'an offer I couldn't refuse.'

In the summer of 1977, during a county match between Somerset and Warwickshire, I had some idea of what was on the cards when Alvin Kallicharran approached me in the dressing room and said that he wanted to talk to me. I had heard through the grapevine that I was going to be approached for a possible world Series Cricket contract.

Kalli and I went to a quiet part of the dressing room. I said, 'OK, Kalli, what is it?'

'Bird,' he asked, 'how would you like to make a lot of money playing cricket?'

I smiled. How would I like to make a lot of money playing cricket indeed. 'What are you talking about?' I asked.

'Well, there is this Australian millionaire, and it looks like he wants to organize some matches among the players. They'd be in Australia and you'd be paid more money than you could ever see from a test match.' Kalli was almost whispering, and I wondered about the need for such secrecy.

'How much are we talking about?' I asked.

'Region of twenty to twenty-five thousand Australian dollars,' Kalli answered.

'For a series of matches?' I asked, raising my voice. 'What do we have to do to earn this sort of money? How many games do we have to play?' I asked Kalli these and other questions.

Kalli's reply was that we would have to do promotions in addition to playing the games. He said that we would have to make personal appearances at different places and described in some detail a public relations plan exposing what we had to offer.

'Does the board know about this?' I asked. I was responding more to the way in which the conversation was being undertaken than from any real concern about the West Indies Cricket Board of Control.

'I don't think so at the moment,' Kalli said, 'but a couple of the lads have already joined up.'

'Like who?' I asked.

'Well, Lloydie is definitely with us,' Kalli said.

He must have known how I would respond to this. The whole team knew that Lloyd and I had become close friends. I respected his point of view on matters extending beyond cricket.

'I'll talk with the skipper and get back to you,' I said.

I thought about the conversation with Kallicharran for a while before I called Lloydie to ask him if he was seriously considering going to Australia with the Packer group. The numbers that Kalli had mentioned were impressive. I thought of the things that I could do with that kind of money. For a start we could do something about the house . . . But first I had to talk to Lloydie.

Lloydie answered immediately when I spoke to him about the conversation I had had with Kallicharran. 'Yeah,' he said, 'I've signed. And a few of the other players have signed too.'

'What about the Board?' I asked.

'I don't see any conflict with the Board,' he said. 'The way I understand the series is organized we won't have any conflict with our commitments to play test cricket for the West Indies. It'll be like playing county or Sheffield Shield cricket, only it'll be a bit more money, that's all. That's the way I look at it.'

'OK,' I said, 'I'm with you.'

'Bird,' Lloydie said; 'Keep things quiet, man.'

'Oh, you know me, man,' I answered.

With that conversation, I committed myself to playing for Kerry Packer's World Series Cricket. I was not then to know what turmoil would follow; but, even if I could have foreseen it, I would have made the same decision. Talking with both Lloydie and the others who had signed provided reasons other than the purely financial for undertaking what we all called 'the experiment'. It was an exciting prospect to play cricket against the world's best. We all agreed that each national team had weak spots that members from other teams could fill. The idea of having the very best in the world compete amongst themselves was also attractive because it would necessarily lead to improved application.

As I remember it, Michael Holding was one of the few who had even the slightest reservations about signing with Packer. He had, apparently, gathered some information from England that South African players had also signed to play 'all over the world'. For Mikey, this meant that he might be bound to play in South Africa, and he had no intention of playing there. It was only the assurances of one of Packer's representatives in Trinidad during the Pakistan tour that convinced him that there would be no obligation to play in South Africa.

I shared Mikey's concerns about playing in South Africa. Lloydie had told me that WSC intended to employ some South African players, most of whom we already played against in county cricket; but that there were no plans to take a team to South Africa. I trusted the skipper's word.

After WSC got under way, we were branded mercenaries, and worse, by the international cricket establishment. Mercenary we might have been, if by that they meant that we were prepared to sell our skill for the highest price (a perspective shared by professionals in every field); but my willingness to play cricket for the highest possible salary stopped where another principle started. In this case, the principle had to do with the appearance of support for the apartheid policies of the South African government. I was not then, and am not now, willing to play cricket there under the conditions that exist for Black people.

If I could go to South Africa and roam the streets as Joel Garner or Big Bird or whatever else people might want to call me, and live under the same conditions that they live under, so that I could share the experience that they have, that would be fair enough; but I am not prepared to accept that status of 'temporary white' while the majority Black population lives under what I consider to be unjust circumstances. I had thought about this for some time and eventually made up my mind when I tried to imagine Barbados being governed by the same kind of laws as those in South Africa. If I had to carry a pass to travel around in the country where I was born, and could only live and work in areas specified by a minority, I don't think that I would like it.

Ironically, the fact that the ban on the Packer players was lifted in such a short time might have influenced some players later to accept contracts to play in South Africa. For myself, the decision to play with WSC was based on a different set of principles to playing in South Africa.

The cricketing establishment did not see the issue in the same light. The controversy started when Kerry Packer tried to get exclusive rights from the Australian Cricket Board of Control for his television channel to cover test cricket in Australia. The Board refused to grant these rights, arguing that it already had a contract with another station and could only consider an offer after the current contract had expired.

Mr Packer set out to establish a parallel series of cricket to test cricket. In June 1977, the International Cricket Conference held an emergency meeting in London to discuss that development. The members decided to meet with Mr Packer, but the subsequent negotiations broke down. In England, the Test and County Cricket Board decided in August that 'No player who, after 1 October 1977, has played or made himself available to play in a match previously disapproved by the Conference shall thereafter be eligible to play in any test match without the express consent of the Conference.'

The decision by the ICC was a unanimous one; but was overthrown in a case brought by three players contracted to play for WSC: Tony Greig, John Snow and Mike Procter. This gave WSC the go-ahead to get started.

After the High Court ruling, West Indian supporters and players looked forward to the best teams representing the two sides to meet in the series scheduled to start in October 1977. The Australian Cricket Board had different ideas. The ruling by the British judge appeared to mean nothing to them and they continued to ostracize the players who had signed up with WSC.

What was taking place in Australia didn't really concern me when, late in 1977, I joined the rest of the West Indian squad to play WSC cricket there. The arrangement was for an Australian team to compete against a World XI and a West Indies XI. Our team comprised: Lloyd (captain), Deryck Murray (vice-captain), Greenidge, Fredericks, Richards, Rowe, Allen, Collis King, Holford, Julien, Roberts, Holding, Daniel, Padmore, and myself. It was arguably the strongest team that could have been mustered in the West Indies at that time. Nine of the eleven who had played the previous test against Pakistan were included. Ironically, Kallicharran, who had been so influential in my signing and who had been the witness to my contract, had withdrawn. Colin Croft had not been approached and I knew that I was going to miss him, because his bowling from the other end in the series against the Pakistanis had been an inspiration.

When I left for Australia, I was concerned that I might not play test cricket again. I had been lucky to gain a place in the side and had performed more creditably than had been predicted by the scribes. I felt that I had secured my place in the team to the extent that even if those players whose injuries had provided the opportunity in the first place had regained fitness, I would still have been chosen. I didn't want to throw away a chance that I had dreamed of for such a long time.

In addition to the fact that recognized top-class players had joined with WSC, I gained strength from the support I got from those who knew me. What struck me was that there was a clear difference in the attitudes towards WSC of two different types of people. One group thought that financial security was secondary to the honour of representing your country. They constantly talked about the traditional standards of the game and how we were about to lower them. These were the ones who most often used the word 'mercenary'. Whenever I overheard that word in conversation, I thought of guerrilla fighters in some jungle fighting for money, and I would give such conversations a wide berth.

On the other hand, there were the people who knew of the upbringing of most of the players and the poor salaries cricketers received. The opportunity to make a decent salary at their job was the first consideration for many of them, including my friends from Enterprise. They wished me good luck when I was about to leave for Australia and gave me their support. They saw the issues as simple folk usually do: as the right to earn a professional wage for a professional job. Most of them thought that this should have been the case long before in West Indies cricket. I felt that I had the full support of the people who mattered most to me. This made me fearless of the consequences and allowed me the luxury of believing that, whatever might happen in Australia, I would play again for the West Indies.

Later developments were to show how much we all needed that kind of support.

When I arrived in Australia for the first WSC season, I was surprised at what I found. We were to play three Supertests against the Australians for the Sir Garfield Sobers trophy. There was also to be an International Cup limited overs competition. This side of the organization was all well and good. But there was another side.

We were to play games at night under lights. We were to play in coloured outfits. The ball would be white. There would be a white circle around the wicket for the limited overs games that would affect field placing for the first fifteen overs. We were to play on grounds that had never previously seen a first-class cricket match.

There was a lot of noise about each of these elements of the WSC game. The players' first priority was the cricket itself. We had made a commitment to play and to make the undertaking work at all costs. What the critics had not borne in mind, as far as our side was concerned, was the background of the majority of the West Indian players. I don't know if any of these features bothered the Aussie or English players. I know that they didn't affect our side in the least. Yes, there was a good deal of ribbing about the coral outfits that we were to wear that turned out to be pink. Anyone with any sense of colour could imagine what a Black man looks like in pink. The moment I put my gear on, the whole dressing room broke up. As for the rest, we could live with that.

In the West Indies, we grew up playing with balls of various colours and sizes when we were too poor to afford the regulation item. A young breadfruit had served many of us as a cricket ball before we were ten years old. White regulation clothes, to my mind, has prevented a number of poor youths in Barbados from participating in various sports. In matches in the roads, we always played in whatever we happened to be wearing at the time. Beach cricket was played wearing only swimming trunks. In Barbados, a cricket field could be anywhere. Many of them are shared with soccer or field-hockey teams. The kind of cricket that most of us had played as poor youngsters prepared us for such a venture as WSC; but the whole organ-

Big Bird flying high.

Aged 11 standing with my brother Bob, aged 6 (*left*).

The house where I grew up during the 1950s and '60s (*middle*).

This is Carter's Gap – referred to as the gap in the book – where I played as a boy (*below*).

Getting established in the highly competitive environment of Barbadian club cricket (*opposite above*).

A breakthrough into the Barbados team – I made my début in the Shell Shield against the Combined Islands in 1975–76 (*opposite below*).

The new arrival under close scrutiny in the nets (*left*).

Ian Botham and Viv Richards congratulate me for bowling Wayne Larkins for 0 in the Gillette Cup final against Northamptonshire in 1979 (*below*).

More encouragement from Botham. This time after I've captured the wicket of Paul Todd in the Benson & Hedges Cup final against Nottinghamshire (*opposite above*).

Somerset fans at the Benson & Hedges final (*opposite right*).

A bear hug for Trevor Gard after he stumped Aslett off Viv Richards in the final of the NatWest Bank Trophy in 1983 (*opposite left*).

BIG BIRD
EATS RICE
FOR
BREAKFAST

A performer in Kerry Packer's circus. (*Left*) Lining up the prey. (*Right*) Sometimes it helps to be tall.

The 1979 World Cup winners.

Meeting the Queen at Lord's on the West Indies' 1980 tour of England.

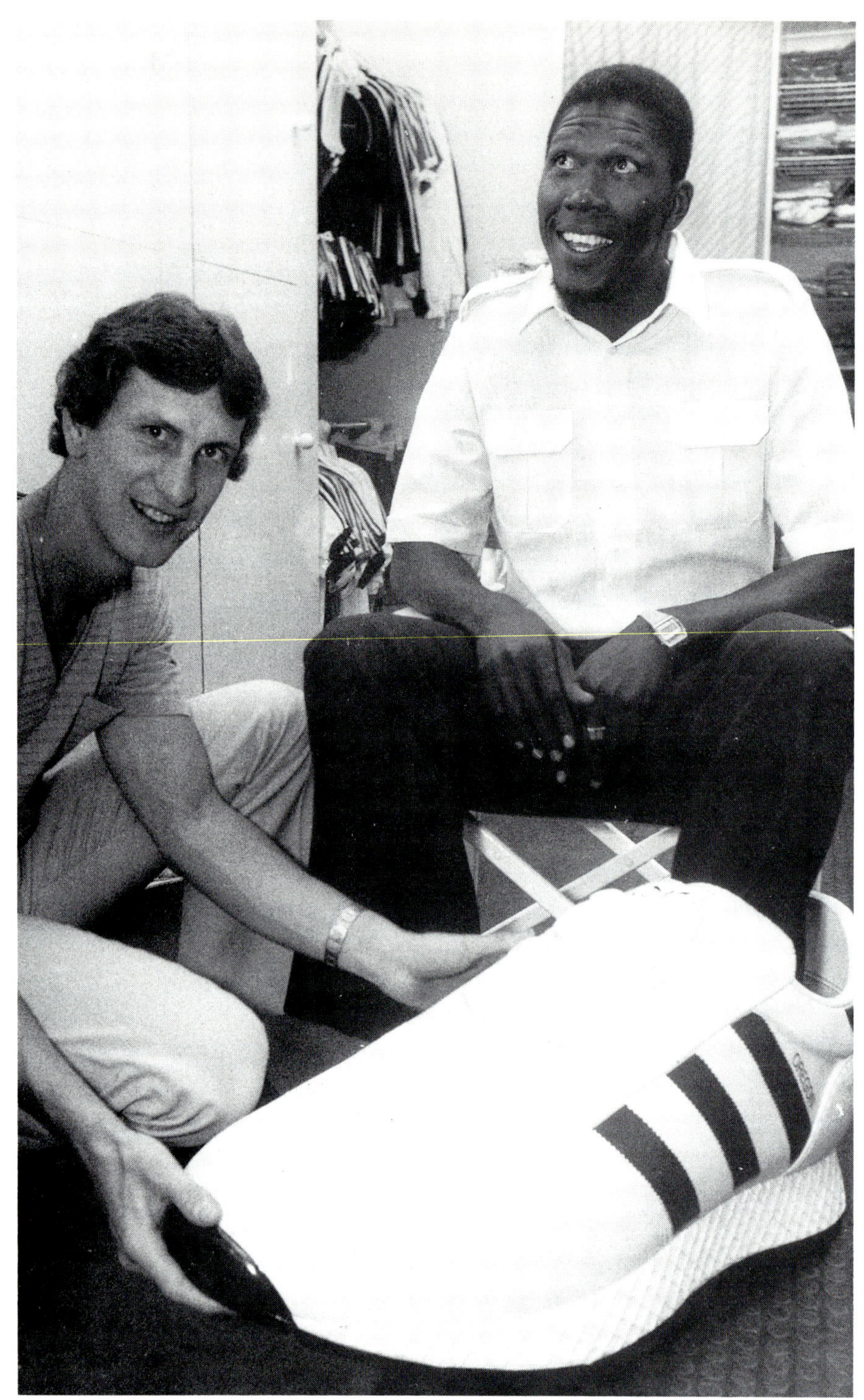

It's never easy to find my size in cricket boots!

ization was strange to those who had worn white outfits and owned quality equipment from the minute they had expressed an interest in the game. The Englishmen, for example, at one stage refused to wear coloured clothing.

The most surprising features of WSC were the level of professionalism expected and the kind of public relations provided. The organizers made it known what they expected. We knew that we were playing for their money, and they in turn expected us to be fit and play to the limit of our abilities. The success of the series depended upon the players' preparation.

A blitz of advertising hit Channel Nine television in Australia. Some players got contracts to advertise various commodities. It was clear from the very start that the WSC organization would go all out to drum up support for the venture. Incidentally, I consider the public relations side to be the most important legacy of WSC. The second most important was the use of multiple cameras to cover a game. This made umpiring decisions more objective because no self-respecting umpire would be careless or biased in a decision that he knew could be instantly replayed in slow motion and carefully analyzed by the public.

As far as WSC promotion was concerned, our cricket Boards in the West Indies could learn a lot from Packer about selling a product. They have taken the fans for granted for too long. They appear unwilling to capture an audience, and are content to put on a show for the faithful to watch.

The West Indian squad during the first WSC series played with deadly seriousness. We considered ourselves a West Indies team, and dedicated ourselves to winning the matches we played. We had the added incentive of prize money; but we always felt that if we lost, we would be disappointing supporters at home. Over the months in Australia, we became a tight-knit unit with great respect for each other's abilities. We knew from reputation and performance that we were up against the very best in the world, and we brought our game up to a corresponding level. Most important, we set out consciously to avenge the defeat that our team had suffered in Australia in 1976.

Australians are never easy opponents. That the Indians were playing test matches against an official team while the WSC series was in progress did nothing to reduce the competitiveness of the WSC Aussies. The cricket was tough; but it was balanced by friendship and goodwill off the field. Rodney Marsh, a close friend for whom I have the greatest respect, was one of cricket's worst raggers. He was a prime example of the way Australians play cricket. They curse you, nag you, stare you down, try every sort of ploy to win a game; and then invite you for a beer when the day is done. For some of our players this was unsettling. It was right up my street.

I would never call another player insulting names, whatever the colour of their skin. In fact, I make it a policy not to talk on the field unless I have to. I don't see my job as engaging in conversation with opposing batsmen. It's to get them out, and the sooner the better. I appreciate the Aussie game and learned a lot about it during the WSC series. Some of my team-mates disliked me socializing with opposing players during the evenings in the bar; but I had my own ideas and did what I thought suited me. Often I had to tell a couple of them that no one could tell me who to drink with.

All the teams stayed in the same hotels, and we got to know each other off the field. There were a number of surprising revelations. I quickly discovered that Marshie is a decent human being! And I suppose the Aussies were shocked to learn that Holding and Roberts could smile and sometimes be downright funny!

The socializing was good, but it was the cricket that mattered. Initially, we were disappointed at the low level of support WSC received from the public. The problem was that the WSC organization had rented huge football grounds far from the cities. We played the first Supertest against the Australians at Victoria Football League Park in Melbourne. The stadium has a capacity of 80,000, but only about 2,000 showed up for the first day of the match. The atmosphere was grim. Another venue would have been better. VFL is about seventeen miles outside Melbourne. Adelaide's Football Park, the other major ground on which we played, seats over 60,000, but is seven miles away from the city.

The spectators were not the only ones put out by the arrangements. The coach trip from the VFL to our hotel took about an hour. Sometimes, the night games finished late. One did not end until after midnight. We got back to the hotel around two in the morning, and had to be ready by 11 am for another match. Constant travel from city to city and promotional activities also drained us. There was none of the relief that we got in a normal test series when we could miss lower level games. When not playing in one of the major games, we found ourselves playing in minor games in various states. We toured the Queensland coast in about two weeks, and played games in places we'd never even heard of: Cairns, Townsville, McKay, Gladstone. On the normal West Indies tour, the team would play only at Brisbane with perhaps a relaxing game at a town like Toowomba, seventy miles away.

I repeat, it was the cricket that mattered; and at that we performed well. Viv Richards showed beyond a shadow of a doubt that he is one of the best. In the six Supertests, he scored 862 runs at an average of 86.2. In all matches, he scored over 1,500 runs in unforgettable fashion. It was a pity that the shadow over WSC prevented some fans from enjoying this master at his very best against talented bowling.

'Smokey' Richards was not the only one to shine during that first WSC series. In Supertest number five at Perth, during three days of the very finest batsmanship, he made 177; but Barry Richards scored 207 and Gordon Greenidge 140 in a World Team total of 625. For Australia, Greg Chappell made a glorious 174. It was unfortunate that this magnificent display was watched by only 3,000 people. But perhaps that is the way it should have been.

This match was an education for me. I was substitute fielder for the World XI. Without going into details, I learned a lot about the kind of bowling certain batsmen like and the sort they dread; and what motives could spur an injured player to incredible feats. I also witnessed the most terrible ragging I have so far heard on a cricket field. Ian Chappell gave Tony Greig the time of his life. He called him all sorts of names. At one point, he raged, 'You're the only player here not deserving to play. You can't bat, you can't bowl. All the others deserve to play, but not you.'

I did not play in the first Supertest; but in the second I began my contributions to the team's success. It was the first time that the Sydney Showground, usually reserved for outdoor events like agricultural shows, was being used for a major cricket match. The curator, John Maley, however, had provided a wicket that was hard and fast. Most of the players felt that it was the best in Australia. I got 3 for 55 in the first innings and 4 for 58 in the second. The West Indies won the game by nine wickets. Once again, the highlight was a masterful 88 by Viv who seemed at one point invincible. I made a sweet little 25 while imagining that I possessed Smokey's talents. Unfortunately for the development of the game and for David Hookes, he was struck in the cheek by a bouncer from Roberts when he had scored 81; he suffered a broken jaw and was out of the match. This severely weakened the Australian batting because David has lots of ability.

In the third Supertest, the Chappell brothers showed that they had no intention of allowing our side to walk all over them. Mainly because of their efforts, Australia beat us by 220 runs with a day to spare at Adelaide's Football Park. Ian made 141 inspired runs before I finally got him to hole out to substitute Jim Allen; and Greg scored 90 to regain his confidence after miserable performances in the previous game. He was mainly responsible for our defeat – with his bowling. He had figures of 5 for 20 off 12 overs in the first innings. In spite of a vintage Richards' innings of 123 in the second innings, we were never really in the game and lost easily. We had won the first two matches, however, and it was a proud Clive Lloyd who accepted the Sir Garfield Sobers trophy from the maestro himself.

I got a further twelve wickets playing for the World XI against the Australians to bring to a satisfactory end a series on which I had gained immense experience. I had bowled against the very best and had survived. I had enjoyed the friendship of the players on the Aussie side as well as on our own. I looked forward to returning to the Caribbean to play against the official Australian team, and had no doubt that the players I had recently met were a cut above the ones that would be on tour. All of us felt that West Indies cricket had been changed by the WSC experience, and we were itching to get back home to prove it.

5

During the WSC series, we were all asked by the West Indies Cricket Board of Control whether we would be available for the 1978 Australian tour of the West Indies. I breathed a sigh of relief because I had seen the treatment that WSC Australians had received and it had made me anxious about what we would have to face when we got back to the Caribbean. Apart from two players, all of us notified the Board that we wanted to play. Roy Fredericks, the talented left-handed batsman, and David Holford, a fine all-rounder, announced their retirement from test cricket. Lloydie was reappointed captain for the five tests, but his wife's ill-health prevented him from returning to the Caribbean for the first limited overs game.

We had every desire to play test cricket, but we knew that certain approaches and conditions in the West Indies had to be changed. During World Series Cricket, we had experienced a high degree of independence. We had begun to think of ourselves as masters of our fate and not under the strict control of any administration. Our behaviour, following from this feeling of independence, confused the Board. The result was that it made a number of ill-considered decisions and announcements.

Gordon Greenidge would, apparently, miss the first test and probably the second because he planned to stay in England for personal reasons. Collis King was chosen for the first one-day international although he could not make it to the Caribbean in time for the game. Kallicharran was omitted from the same game on the understanding that he would not be back home soon enough. The selectors, on the eve of the game, had to replace King with Kallicharran; and Greenidge was back in time for the first test.

The first sign that the Board's loosening control over us was going to cause problems came with the selection of the team for the one-day international. With Lloyd still in England, Deryck Murray, who had been vice-captain, was appointed skipper for the game in Antigua. He later protested that he had played no part in choosing the team he was supposed to lead, but had been presented with the names of the players – down to the twelfth man.

The Board badly misjudged the attitudes of some of the key players. I feel that the selectors' treatment of Murray was responsible for the protest he and Richards staged by wearing their red WSC caps while playing the limited overs game. Board members who remarked on this interpreted it as an insult to West Indies cricket. I suppose that both Murray and Richards knew that there would be some kind of reaction from the Board, but neither of them could know when or how it would come.

We were all concerned about the worsening relations with the Board; but there was a more important job to do. We wanted revenge for the beating the Aussies had given us in 1976. In spite of our success against strong teams on the WSC tour, we considered test cricket to be special. We saw the Packer series as a chance to make money, not as a replacement for test cricket. Defeating the Australians under the auspices of WSC meant less to us than beating them in an official test series.

In the first one-day game, we nearly failed. We found the going a bit rough, losing the top five wickets quickly for 121. Desmond Haynes, in his first international appearance, played a mature and exciting innings after a shaky start. He hit 2 sixes and 16 fours in 148 runs off only 136 balls. In our fifty overs, we made 313 runs. Even if the light had not been as bad as it was by the time we were all out, the game was beyond Australia's reach. I enjoyed bowling with Croft again, and when play was stopped we had figures of 3 for 44 and 3 for 29, respectively. Australia were restricted to 181 for 7 and we won because of a better scoring rate.

At the team meeting before the first test in Trinidad, we agreed that the Australian team was much weaker than it could have been because of their Board's refusal to select WSC players. Bobby Simpson had been recalled from the series against India to captain the side; but we felt that the general standard of cricket had greatly improved in the ten years since his retirement. Lloyd nevertheless stressed that no Australian team should be underestimated. He argued that they wanted to beat us as much as we wanted to beat them, if only to justify their selection.

We had two good reasons why we wanted to beat this particular Australian side. One was simply revenge. The other was that if we should lose to the replacements for the WSC players, we would have undermined WSC cricket and our own standing as professional players.

On the first morning of the test, the rain fell constantly and delayed the start of the game. Only one over was possible before lunch. Lloyd won the toss and sent the Australians in to bat on an unpredictable wicket. The batsmen watching for the pavilion must have been disheartened by what they saw. Roberts' second delivery to Serjeant lifted sharply and struck the handle of the bat, the second slowed after it pitched, beat Wood and went past Murray on the second bounce for four byes. Whilst the rain had been falling, there was time for reflection on the decision of the selectors to appoint Richards as vice-captain when Murray was still in the side. This decision was only relayed to the team on the morning of the game and did not go down very well with the players, some of whom thought that the selectors were obviously playing one off against the other.

The players respected both Murray and Richards. Those of us who had played in the WSC series had come to regard status within the team as secondary to performance. We really couldn't care less who was vice-captain. We were prepared to go out to the middle and work as hard as we could at our jobs. But we did care how other players were treated, and the feeling grew that Murray was being victimized because he was a recruiting agent for WSC. We came to a consensus that we would ignore the Board's pettiness and play as hard as we could.

After the break, Colin bowled five overs before conceding a run, and by then he had dismissed both Wood and Yallop. Only Cosier put up any defence against us. He scored an admirable 46 after watching Toohey, in attempting a courageous (or foolhardy) hook, suffer a nasty blow to his right eye. He himself had a Roberts' bouncer glance off his head and race to the boundary at fine leg. The rest of the Aussie batsmen put up a dismal show and they were all out for 90 runs in 36 overs; the lowest total ever recorded in a test at the ground.

As often happens when the weather changes as much as it had done in the morning, by afternoon the moisture had gone out of the wicket and in an hour or so before close of play Haynes and Greenidge scored 79 brisk runs. Haynes in particular was brutal against the fast bowling. Given Thompson's reputation, it was surprising to see him treated as he was. Desmond took twenty off one exciting over, including a hook for six from a no-ball, and was 53 at the close on the first day.

The following day, Thomson seemed keen to prove that what had happened the previous afternoon was unusual. He bowled very quickly and accurately; but after Greenidge and Haynes were out, Kallicharran and Lloyd took the score to 313 for 3 at tea. But some Australian player must have had his prayers answered during the interval. Crickus made his presence felt immediately afterwards, and we added only 78 runs while losing six wickets. Only Kalli put up any resistance to the attack. He was finally out for 127 when he wearily drove over an off-break from Yardley.

We were over 300 runs in the lead on the third day, but Lloyd decided to bat on. It took only a quarter of an hour before Croft was out, and the Australians faced as difficult a job as cricket could provide. Yallop played a wonderful knock of 81, but after he left there was a continual procession from the Australian dressing room. Roberts bowled as well as he could, and finally ended the Australian agony when he mercifully knocked Higgs' stumps from behind him, with Toohey in the pavilion being out injured from the first innings.

We won the game by an innings and 106 runs. I had match figures of 5 for 74, Croft 4 for 70 (all in the first innings) and Roberts 7 for 82, five from the second innings, four of which came in one blistering spell at the end of the game. The West Indies performance showed how much the WSC players had learned in Australia. In the first innings, six Australian batsmen were caught off fast bowlers while the wicket had an uneven bounce. This meant that the fielders, especially those in the slips, were doing better than many a West Indian team had done before. In the second innings, all the Aussie batsmen were either clean bowled or lbw. Haynes and Murray had made the greatest contributions to our victory apart from Kallicharran's century and Roberts' bowling in the second innings.

During the second test at Kensington, developments off the field were as important as action on it. One of Mr Packer's representatives arrived from Australia to try to sign three more players for the second season of World Series Cricket. There had been only fifteen in the original group. We knew that with the exacting itinerary we would have to retain more players or risk unnecessary injury and become stale and tired. He approached Desmond Haynes, Colin Croft and Richard Austin who was a useful all-rounder who could help Collis King by taking some pressure off the number seven position. By the end of the Kensington test, all three had signed with WSC. This meant that nine of us playing the test were WSC professionals. This fact could not have been lost on a Board becoming increasingly suspicious of our intentions.

We won the second test in three days; but it was a very close contest. The main difference between the two teams was that the Australian batting failed once more against our fast bowling. I had match figures of 8 for 121, Croft 5 for 100, and Roberts 5 for 129. Wood was run out in the second innings. We three had accounted for all of the wickets that had fallen to bowlers. The Aussie's poor performance was unexpected because immediately before the test they had done well against a strong Barbados team, scoring 511 on the wicket next to the test wicket. Simpson and Serjeant both scored centuries in the island game but then both failed in the test.

The wicket for the test was greener than we had come to expect at Kensington. Lloyd won the toss and sent the Aussies in. After an early breakthrough, Wood and Yallop batted confidently until lunch. After the break, with Wood on 69 and Yallop on 30, the Australian position got worse and worse. Croft got two quick wickets to make the score 134 for 4, and then scared Simpson out of his wits with a ball that reared into his face and which he could only edge to the keeper while protecting himself. Cosier followed in much the same way, but to Roberts. Yardley swung his bat for 74 useful runs, playing some most unorthodox shots. He square cut and hooked two consecutive deliveries from yours truly for sixes. He was the last man out. Before he left, I concentrated on bowling fast and straight and took all four of the tail-end wickets to fall. The Australians had made exactly 250 and we felt pleased with the job we had done when we walked off the field with just over an hour left to play.

That afternoon the West Indian players and the Kensington crowd watched with admiration and respect at a spell of fast bowling that appeared all the more fantastic for being unexpected. We had heard how fearsome Jeff Thomson had been in Australia in 1976; but after Desmond Haynes had manhandled him in Trinidad it was thought that he might have been losing some of his sting. Thomson showed us that Saturday afternoon that he was still far from ready to retire to the Australian surf. Greenidge, Richards and Kallicharran were among the best batsmen in the world. I sat in wonder and astonishment as Thomson made them look like amateurs.

In his first over, Thomson struck Greenidge with a wicked bouncer that swung into the batsman off the wicket. A loud appeal for a catch behind off the glove was turned down, and this appeared to send Thommo crazy. In the third over, he produced a carbon copy delivery and Gordon was caught at second slip, and you could imagine how the crowd reacted.

Viv Richards does not like to be intimidated. He plays his cricket as aggressively as anyone. We sat back in the pavilion to watch what we knew would be an interesting duel. Viv, attempting a pull shot, was dropped at backward square leg before he had scored. Thomson came back with a bouncer pitched on a good length and aimed straight at the body. Viv was struck hard on the shoulder. I would rate the following over from Thomson to Richards as good as any a fast bowler ever delivered.

The over included four no-balls, always a sign that a quickie is seeking that extra pace; a hook for six; a straight drive back overhead for four and, off the last ball, a full-blooded hook that Clark took at deep fine leg in spectacular fashion. I think that the two players' respect for each other increased a thousand per cent after that over.

Really fast bowlers and good batsmen are not opposites. They are two elements in the same system. They balance each other. It is because I believe this that I would rather bowl at Richards, Chappell or Botham than at a host of lesser players. Bowling against a talented player raises a bowler's game. When I have to bowl for an extended period, I regard it as a game of cat and mouse: an intrigue where I work out my strategy to counter what I think the batsman will attempt to do. I have taken some of the best batsmen's wickets by thinking them out. Few of them are without weaknesses, and I've found that the best time to exploit any weaknesses is at the start of their innings. If the batsman is slightly reckless or has a carefree disposition, it is good strategy to tie him up early in his innings.

The bouncer is a central part of a fast bowler's strategy. Most of the noise about the number of short-pitched deliveries West Indies fast bowlers deliver comes from those who don't think about the game a great deal. If batsmen like Botham, Richards, Gooch, Gower and Border knew that you couldn't bowl short at them, they'd murder you. The rest of the noise comes from self-serving patriots. There were no complaints about bouncers in the English press when Trueman, Tyson and Snow were letting fly. There were few opponents of the short-pitched ball in Australia when Lindwall and Miller, and later Lillee and Thomson, were having a go. These players were national heroes – and so they should be.

A bouncer is nothing but a fast bowler's strike weapon. To deprive him of it, or to limit the number he may bowl, is to give the batsman an unfair advantage. After all, test players are supposed to be the best in the world. I don't think that a batsman deserves to be rated as a test player if he can't hit or avoid a sharply-rising delivery. If the number of bouncers per over is limited, the sound batsman could move forward on to the front foot after the number of short deliveries has been bowled and comfortably play most of the quickies he's ever likely to face.

In any case, on that Saturday afternoon at Kensington, Thomson was demonstrating fast bowling at its best. When Kallicharran weakly pushed at the last ball of the day and was caught at close backward short leg off his glove, Thommo had taken 3 for 40; we were 71 for 3, the game was evenly balanced, and the fans had been given an essay in the effective use of the new ball. They packed the ground the following day, no doubt because they had heard what Thomson had done the previous afternoon and came to see for themselves.

Unfortunately, their hero strained a muscle in his calf, bowled only three half-paced overs at the start of play, and retired to the dressing room well before lunch. Haynes, Lloyd and Austin went by the time our score was 198. Murray played a solid knock before Thomson returned and deepened the impact he had already made on the match. He cleaned up the last three wickets and finished with figures of 6 for 77, the best for an Australian bowler in Barbados. He deserved the standing ovation the Barbadian fans gave him. It was a splendid performance by a marvellous bowler.

Cricket is, of course, a game of batting as well as bowling, and the tired Thomson must have been dejected watching his team-mates in the two and a half hours that remained for play on the second day. By close of play, they had made only 96 runs while losing 5 wickets and their lead was 58. Roberts was our strike bowler, and he must have known that comparison with Thomson was unavoidable. He took three quick wickets on that afternoon, bowling extremely quickly and getting the ball to bounce with a venom that put off all the early batsmen.

On the third morning, Wood, who had made 55 while Roberts blasted away, was run out in the third over and the Australian innings became a shambles. Only Yardley, clobbering the ball as hard as he had done in the first innings, showed any resistance. They were all out for 178, with Clark scoring his fourth duck in as many innings.

With 141 to win and all the time in the world, Greenidge and Haynes treated the hometown crowd to the sort of batting display Barbadians love. Haynes swung Yardley for two successive sixes and in addition struck 5 fours in a dashing 55. Greenidge was a little less carefree, yet managed to hit the same bowler straight for another six and included 11 fours in his 80 not out.

This was the first time that an Australian–West Indies test at Kensington had ended in a result. All three previous games had been drawn. The greenness of the wicket on the first day and the efforts of the fast bowlers, especially Thomson and Roberts, contributed to the outcome. In our dressing room at the end of the game, we congratulated each other and had special pats on the back for Haynes, who scored 66 and 55, and Murray who, in addition to a fine innings of 60 that changed the course of the game, held six catches.

Imagine our surprise when we learned the day before the third test was to begin that Murray and Haynes had been dropped from the side. It seemed to us that the storm which had been brewing behind the scenes had taken its first victims. We discussed the developments and came to the conclusion that if we did nothing then it would carry away a few more.

When the selectors dropped three of the WSC players for the third test against the Australians, it brought to a head the conflict that had been brewing between the Board and the players from the time the Packer series was first mentioned. The players began to distrust the Board when they felt that it was inconsistent in dealing with the WSC issue. The West Indies Board had voted at the ICC meeting in London in favour of the resolution calling for a ban on the Packer players; then it had reassured us that they had done so in order to maintain unity in the international organization. They had been the only test match playing Board not to have carried out the ban on their players involved with WSC.

Because communication with the players had almost completely broken down, a number of misunderstandings occurred and the Board had become more and more insecure about its hold over us. Some members began to suspect our motives, and saw any decision we made as a sign of growing militancy. This could have been the way they interpreted Bernard Julien's decision not to play for Trinidad against Australia, although it had been taken for purely personal reasons about which they had been informed.

Our manager and the captain had both suggested that I should be rested for the Barbados game. The message was supposed to be relayed to the chairman of selectors for the Barbados team; but the next thing I knew was that 'sources' were informing the press that I didn't like playing for my island. This hurt so much that, to this day, I have not forgotten the persons involved for not telling the public the truth.

Given our relations with the Board, we had expected strange selection procedures. Nevertheless, we found it hard to understand why Jim Allen, a WSC player, had been omitted from the one-day international. We also felt that Douglas Sang Hue was not asked to umpire after the first test because of his contract with WSC.

With the general atmosphere as heavy as it was, when the

three players signed their WSC contracts during the second test the Board obviously felt this was the last straw and decided to treat World Series Cricket and its players more firmly than before. The Board claimed that the three players had given their word that they would not sign another contract until the Board came up with an alternative. This never happened, although the Board later made a statement that they considered the players' action to be a breach of trust.

An issue was made out of the West Indies tour to India which was scheduled for later that year. Murray, the secretary of the Player's Association, received a letter from the Board asking him to indicate if the WSC players would be available for the tour. We considered this an unusual request because it affected only specific players; but we contacted the Packer organization and explained our situation. We were told that WSC was in the process of negotiating with the Indian Board to try to change the dates of the West Indies tour so that both sets of games could be played. Murray then wrote to our Board and asked for an extension of the deadline they had given him for a commitment to the Indian tour.

Although I was aware of the problems with the Board, I was still surprised when I arrived in Georgetown for the third test and a hopping mad Clive Lloyd called to tell me that he had resigned from the captaincy. We had a long conversation but he was so angry that he could hardly contain himself. He told me in no uncertain terms that he could not agree to change a team that had beaten the Australians so thoroughly in two tests. He said that Murray and Haynes had performed better than could have been expected of them, and that Austin had not really been given a chance to prove himself. He referred to the incident in the second test when the vice-captain had been changed without his knowledge and argued that the whole affair was a return to the way that West Indies teams used to be picked. In those days the islands would fight amongst themselves for their respective nationals to be chosen without regard to the balance of the team as a whole. Lloyd felt that it was a matter of principle that the West Indies should be represented by its strongest and most professional side in all tests. He finished by telling me that, since he did not agree with the team, he had not signed the press release naming its members.

I agreed with all that Lloyd had to say. I told him that if he was not going to be playing, then I didn't think that any of the others would be playing either. I felt that the time had come to take a stand against what we thought was the selectors' open attempt to intimidate players. He said that that was a decision for the rest of us to make, but that as far as he was concerned he had had enough.

Much to our surprise, in spite of the fact that there was a strike affecting BWIA, the regional airline, we later found out that most of the players who were to replace us for the third test were 'holidaying' in Guyana at the same time as we were supposed to be playing there. We didn't think that this was a coincidence. We went to a meeting with the Board and when we got back to the Pegasus Hotel we discovered that we were no longer registered there, nor were there alternative plans for our accommodation or transportation. As far as the Board was concerned, we were on our own.

Greenidge and I got in touch with all the members of the team. Andy Roberts and Viv Richards were in Antigua and were easy to contact. They agreed not to play in the test. We first had to convince them that neither of us would be playing, because they wanted to know what we were still doing in Guyana if we were serious. The other players were scattered throughout the islands, but we reached them one by one and sometimes had as many as four of them on different lines at the same time. Finally, and mainly because we gave our word to each of them, they all agreed not to play in the third test.

The WSC players trusted Clive Lloyd, and this was the major reason for our decision. There was also a second reason. Most of us who had gone on the first WSC tour had expected some unfavourable reaction from the Board. In Australia, we had all felt that at any time we would learn that we had been banned from test cricket. Because we were psychologically prepared, I suppose it was easier for us to step out of the team than it would have been for the Board to sack us.

After I had made up my mind not to play, I felt great relief. I had seen how the WSC Australians had been treated in Australia. At the time I thought that we were lucky not to have been banned; but I was uncomfortable to have a drink with Australian friends who were being rejected, in some instances

by people who had appeared to be close friends less than a year
before.

When our players refused to play in the third test in Guyana,
there was no WSC player left in test cricket. The cricketers who
were reputedly the best in the world were unable to represent
their countries. I wondered how long the fans would accept such
a situation. In the West Indies, they did not take it for long.
The third test itself was played, from all reports, to a packed
house and unexpectedly without incident. In Trinidad, on the
other hand, a group calling itself the Committee in Defence of
West Indies Cricket organized a boycott of the fourth test. The
attendance for the game at Queen's Park Oval reached only
3,000 each day. I don't know if this was a result of the boycott
or the fact that even Crickus didn't seem to like what was going
on: the West Indies replacements had lost the third test in
Guyana to the Australian replacements. By that time, I really
couldn't care less. I was angry at the way the Board had treated
the players, and the way that they had obviously planned their
action. I felt that I finally knew whom Gran had meant when
she constantly told me to watch out for 'them'.

After spending an enjoyable weekend at the Sandy Lane
Hotel in Barbados with the other WSC players and their families, courtesy of Mr Kerry Packer, and discussing plans for a
WSC tour of the West Indies during the 1979 season, I packed
my bags and left for England to fulfil my League cricket obli-
gations. The issue was resolved. I was not going to play for the
official West Indies team again and that was that. I drew
consolation from the fact that any cricket I played would be
against the very best players and for a salary that my ability
justified. I flew into the English cold with relief. I was a few
pounds lighter. Batsmen were going to have to watch out.

On the flight to England, much as I tried to concentrate on
what awaited me at the other end and however hard I tried to
finish the Wilbur Smith novel I was reading, I kept thinking
about what it would mean not to play test cricket again. I
couldn't believe that it was all over. I tried to think of the
possible developments that would enable me to wear the West
Indies sweater once more. I knew that the West Indians had
protested against the team that was completing the series

against the Australians. I felt that they would have been better off demonstrating against the years of shoddy treatment the Board had dished out to the players, and the insularity that affected the majority of selection decisions. Unhappily, I told myself that the Board's behaviour had not been unusual. In the past, the spectators had done little about it.

I made up my mind that if my test career was at an end, I owed it to myself to raise my professional game to the highest level, if only to ensure that I would continue in employment. Much had happened in a year. When I had gone to Australia, the Board had said little about their plans for WSC players. Now, it looked as though we were going to be out in the cold.

On arrival in Manchester, I found that the Central Lancashire League had its own problems. There were falling receipts at the gates and from club membership. The League sent out feelers to the Lancashire League about the possibility of a merger; but its representatives were informed that that was out of the question. The Lancashire League had a unique atmosphere because its fixtures were local clashes among fourteen clubs within about a twenty-mile radius. This was what gave the League its fanatical support, and its reputation for keen competition. They were not prepared to give this up to help the stricken Central Lancashire League.

These problems didn't affect me as much as those in the West Indies. During the season, my performance improved from game to game. I bowled as if my livelihood depended upon it. I had a WSC contract, but there was no way of knowing whether there would be a second tour, or how many after that. I was probably responsible for Littleborough's domination of the League that year. We won only one more game than Walsden, but were always a force to be reckoned with, and finished the season a clear eight points ahead of them. I took 119 wickets at an average of 6.7. The closest bowler to me among the professionals was Derek Parker at Ashton, who got 106 at 11.75 each. A few of the umpires did not share my attitude towards the short-pitched delivery and I ran into some opposition from them on a couple of occasions. But there was never really any doubt about us winning the championship.

I was pleased with Littleborough's performance. It brought out that our success the previous year had not been a fluke. We had come first then, also. I had taken 105 wickets at an average of **8.54**. Ashton had come second, and Derek Parker had taken 130 wickets at **8.84** with his mixture of leg-spin and seam bowling. At the end of the season, I had completed my contract with Littleborough and in 1979 I would be moving south to play full-time for Somerset. I remain grateful to the players and spectators at Littleborough. I feel that they missed me too because later, when I checked their performance for 1979, I noticed that they had fallen to the middle of the standings.

There are times now when I remember with greater appreciation some of the conditions and experiences I had while playing with Littleborough, and I always smile. All in all, I enjoyed my stay with the club. It was a good team to begin a first-class career with. I feel I owe them a lot because without them I might never have played for the West Indies.

During my mid-week outings for Somerset, in spite of suffering from torn muscle fibres in my side, I managed to top their bowling averages with **22** wickets at **15.95** per wicket, in four games. Brian Rose had become captain of the team and the players were visibly relieved not to have Brian Close at the helm. This was reflected in their play. With the youngest team in their history, the club experienced its best season. Somerset came fifth in the championship, second in the John Player League, were Gillette Cup finalists, and semi-finalists in the Benson and Hedges Cup.

By the end of the English season, although I had chatted with Viv Richards about it on many occasions, I had put the problems of West Indies cricket behind me. I jumped on the carousel that my cricket career had become and rushed off to Australia for the second production of World Series Cricket.

I had looked forward to playing in Australia again; and so, I think, had the other members of the side. During the previous outing we had performed at a very high level and had come to feel at home in Australian surroundings. The Aussies had a distinctly more 'Caribbean' approach to life than the English. They played their cricket hard; but they were a high-spirited people with a love of life that I found attractive. As far as the cricket was concerned, I felt that we could at least repeat our performances on the field, although I was not at all sure about how we would react to the pressure that the hectic schedule would place on us.

As it turned out, the second series of World Series Cricket was far tougher for us than the first. We struggled against injuries, lack of form of some of our key players, and lost two of the three Supertests and drew the other. It was also abundantly clear that the opposition was much better prepared this time than on the previous occasion. After qualifying for the Grand Finals of the limited overs International Cup Competition only by virtue of a marginally better overall scoring rate than the World Team, we showed some competitive spirit by taking the best of five competition three-one, after losing the first game.

Overall, we were not the same team that had come to Australia the year before. The other teams had, during the intervening period, studied video tapes of our past games to analyze our strengths and weaknesses. They therefore presented more difficulties than we had expected. For our part, some of our players had been disappointed by the low number of spectators at World Series Cricket the previous season; others were more than a little dejected at the prospect of being ruled out of test cricket for the foreseeable future. There was a feeling of depression in the dressing room. Unfortunately for the paying public, what they saw during this season was not what they had come to expect from West Indies cricket.

Most of us played that series as if in a daze, and we could not blame the weather, the kind of cricket or the locations. We had become accustomed to all of these factors. I think that what really affected us was a kind of guilt. We felt that we had done something wrong. We had a lot of confidence in World Series Cricket; but even with the greatest confidence and a full appreciation of the principle that lay behind what we were doing, we remained at heart West Indies players. I felt that this meant that we should be playing West Indies test cricket. We all began to appreciate more fully what the Australian players had had to put up with during that first season of WSC when they were out in the cold.

Ironically, as dejection tightened its grip on our side, the Australians got a boost by way of approval to play at the Sydney Cricket Ground and at Brisbane. These were the first traditional test venues we were allowed to play at, and the availability of these grounds must have made them feel that they were no longer the pariahs of Australian cricket. On the other hand, we were playing badly. I remember that while playing at Sydney, we got bowled out for **66** and were told off by Mr Packer himself and punished by having to play two games on the same day. If tables could ever be completely turned, this was certainly a prime example. During the first series of World Series Cricket, the West Indies team had not been banned from test cricket and the Aussies had been. Now, we faced the likelihood of not playing again for our national side while they were being given signals that they might soon be taken back into the fold.

Surely the injuries we suffered during that tour could not all have been psychosomatic; but we did have more than our fair share. Hardly anyone was spared, and the selectors could seldom choose the best team. Deryck Murray dislocated his shoulder in a fielding collision with Colin Croft and was forced to miss the Supertest preliminary against the World team and several International Cup games. When he did return, he was quickly put out of action again with a knee injury, and his batting suffered as a result. Roy Fredericks, our gifted opening batsman, could not play in either of the Supertests against Australia because of a broken finger sustained at net practice. Desmond Haynes, in his first season with WSC, just as he appeared to be finding his natural form which would have been a major help to us, unfortunately tore ligaments in his left hand and was out of the game for the last three weeks of the season. Collis King fell victim to his habit of batting without a thigh pad and missed several matches. I myself was retired to the dressing room for a couple of weeks while I waited for strained side muscles to regain full strength.

Our most serious injury was Mikey Holding's which happened early in the Supertest against the World team. He snapped his right hamstring and could not play again for a month. When he did return, for the first two games in the International Cup grand finals, the injury was not fully healed and he had to withdraw. Suprisingly, for a while it looked as though only Lawrence Rowe, the Jamaican batsman who until then had been particularly injury prone, would survive unhurt. He really struck form and batted for a short while with all the elegance and ease and ability he had shown earlier in the seventies. His innings of 85 in the Supertest followed by 175 against the Australians were batting displays of the highest quality. Then he too fell: a victim of influenza. His batting deteriorated rapidly and disappointingly. His century, however, was the only hundred by a West Indian player in the Supertests, and one of only four in the series; the others being by Richards, Jim Allen, and Fredericks in county matches against the Cavaliers.

That the Australians were hampered by a string of low scores was only some consolation. The WSC, test series and Sheffield Shield all reflected low scores. This could not be blamed on a general and uniform fall in the standard of pitch preparation that year. With the preponderance of very fast bowling in the WSC group, though the other teams were improving quickly, one could expect low scores.

There was a general feeling, something undefinable, that you couldn't even talk about for fear that you would, by speaking, have applied a pin to the balloon of our pretended confidence. For me, the feeling had something to do with ambition and national pride. I had become more realistic, more cynical; both as far as cricket and gaining national glory through playing it were concerned. I missed playing for the West Indies. I knew that I could just as easily have been playing for South Point or YMPC or Littleborough; it was just that I had thought that being selected for the West Indies would be the high point of my cricketing career, and here I was playing in a kind of game that would certainly guarantee that I would never represent the West Indies again. I remain convinced that, had the West Indies Cricket Board announced before the second WSC tour that we were eligible to play for the test side, the standard of cricket, at least for our team, would have been much higher.

It was sad that we should perform as we did during this series because we had done so remarkably well during the first tour. Ironically, when the cricket was better, we had had extremely low attendances; and now that we were worse, an enormous number of people seemed suddenly to be interested in WSC. Obviously, permission to use test match venues rather than fairgrounds helped a great deal. Despite the simultaneous presence of the Ashes series, WSC managed to increase gates significantly. The average attendance at city matches was 10,000 a day, and on three occasions it was more than 30,000. This was a far cry from the 1977–8 series when the large stadiums in which we played had been embarrassingly empty.

While we were at a low ebb as far as relations with our Board were concerned, the Aussies were approaching high tide. Whereas in the first year there had been little identification of Ian Chappell's WSC Australians as a national team, there was now little doubt that they were the national side. Australian flags waved every time a wicket fell or a boundary was struck. Banners and streamers around the grounds proclaimed the heroes of the moment. The chants when Lillee charged ferociously in to bowl were as frenzied as any in the days when he represented the official team.

The most important changes came from new promotional tactics used by the WSC organizers. One of the early taunts against WSC was that the teams that were playing had no real national identity, especially the Australians, and this had accounted for the kind of treatment they had received during the first tour. We were seen as playing not for honour or country but for money. This, though to a large extent true, was changed by the WSC promotional people. They began to focus in their advertisements upon the training programme in which the Australians had engaged during the winter; they devised a catchy little jingle urging, 'C'mon, Aussie, c'mon' to whip up patriotic fervour, and used television to good effect. Channel Nine's advertising was dramatic: a mixture of the Italian western with close-ups, danger men and suspenseful action and the fabricated confrontation of good and evil. For a brief moment, cricket had completed the Atlantic crossing and had symbolically reached Hollywood.

During the first tour the Australians had disappointed a public that does not take kindly to losing; and they showed that they were determined not to let it happen again. The fans were right behind them, shouting 'C'mon, Aussie, c'mon.' The cheer-leading song became as popular as 'Those pals of mine, Ramadhin and Valentine' had become in the West Indies in the fifties. It became a number one hit and was even chanted at the official tests.

WSC won the day through its aggressive marketing. Disregarding the assumption that cricket would sell itself and that public interest would be generated by the occasional good press, WSC ran full-page ads, bought posters on buses and trams and billboards, and saturated Channel Nine with the message: 'Come See The White Ball Fly!' 'Big Boys Play at Night!' 'Supertests! Superstars!' The sponsors utilized the selling power of the players. Wayne Daniel tried to seduce viewers into buying MacDonalds hamburgers and Dennis Lillie urged them to hire a car from one company rather than another.

And then, right in the middle of it all when we were at our lowest and feeling that perhaps it was not worth it at all; when playing cricket seemed more like a sentence to everlasting damnation than something we enjoyed; and when we had reached the point from which we couldn't go on any more, we received letters from the West Indies Board of Control asking whether we would be available for the World Cup Tournament in England, scheduled for the following June.

Phew!

6

I returned to the Caribbean with the rest of the WSC players after what was a terribly exhausting series in Australia. Certain developments outside the cricket arena threatened severe repercussions on the third WSC series which we were scheduled to play against the Australians in the West Indies. The planned itinerary included five Supertests and twelve one-day matches; and, although the two teams were considered the best that their countries could produce, this served as little protection against the fatigue that set in among the players, most of whom had played cricket almost continually for a year.

I have already said that in the West Indies cricket is much more than a sport. This fact cannot be overemphasized. The game provides the raw material of folk-lore and it gives the stauncher supporters their sense of identify in a country composed of separate and disparate island states. It binds together a group of insular territories that, in the aftermath of an aborted attempt at federation, could find very little in the way of social glue. I will never forget how I felt when I saw a grown West Indian lying on the field at Lord's and crying like a baby after we had lost the World Cup final to India in 1983. It does not surprise me that social and political events have clear manifestations among spectators at cricket games in the Caribbean.

During the 1970s the international energy crisis had adversely affected most of the Caribbean islands. Trinidad, which produces its own oil, was the only island to withstand the ravages of spiralling costs. Inevitably, this led to increases in the levels of unemployment and signs of growing frustration among the various populations. Anti-social behaviour, mainly in the form of crime and disrespect for authority, was on the increase throughout the region. In Grenada there had been a left-wing coup which removed an elected government and replaced it with one that was later to openly declare its affiliations with international socialism. Cricket's administrators in the islands would have been short-sighted if they took no account of these developments. Apart from carnivals of various types, cricket commands greater popular support in the West Indies than any other social event. If there is an underlying current of dissatisfaction, one would least expect it to surface at a cricket game.

Unpredictably, disorder struck the World Series games in the West Indies in 1979. For the first time in the placid history of the staid Kensington Oval in Barbados, there were crowd disturbances. Spectators also stopped play in Trinidad; and the crowd came perilously close to a full-scale riot in Guyana. Doubtless, the general social and political situation formed the background to the events, but the immediate causes were much simpler: unfavourable umpiring decisions, unexplained stoppages, poor amenities at most grounds, and a wide gulf between the majority of the spectators that support West Indies cricket and the few individuals who run it.

I feel that I should stress that it was the social issues which were the primary cause of the problems because there have been unpopular decisions before in the West Indies that have passed without incident. There have also been frequent stoppages for rain that spectators have accepted quietly. For reasons that must have something to do with the history of the game in the Caribbean, cricket is played there in the rainy season. There are times when play is stopped for a drizzle that would be considered normal playing conditions in England. Amenities at the various pavilions have not suddenly become poor; but they have deteriorated over a period of time. Many of the problems of crowd control at West Indies cricket games could be avoided if the authorities improved their public relations and informed the spectators that discretion was being used concerning the state of the outfield and that they were protecting the fitness of the players and trying to avoid potential injury by preventing players running on saturated grounds.

Certainly one way of reducing the probability of a reoccurrence of unpleasant crowd behaviour would be for the West Indies cricket authorities to show more courtesy to the spectators. After all, the West Indies fan is about the most knowledgeable about cricket in the world. But in the final analysis, if crowds are frustrated and want to misbehave during a cricket match then there is nothing that an administration can do to prevent unpleasantness without increasing restrictive measures at the grounds. There has been some talk over the years about banning alcohol at games. I think that this is a joke. Four out of six men at a cricket game in the West Indies have a drink during a day's play. There are rarely acts of violence simply because of this. West Indian crowds are usually very noisy while watching cricket. Shouting instructions or criticisms to players on the field is their way of getting involved in the game; and sometimes I think that this is misinterpreted as rowdiness.

During the WSC series in the West Indies, the organization of the series itself gave grounds for concern. The spectators had given World Series Cricket great support in the face of the Board's opposition, and had approved of the players' stance in quitting during the previous test series against Australia. They had high expectations of the scheduled games but had not perhaps considered that the players were exhausted. They had not thought the 1978 Bobby Simpson team a representative Australian side, and therefore they looked to the WSC tour to finally provide the revenge for the humiliation of 1976. Dennis Lillee and Jeff Thomson were to be together again, since Thomson had been released from his Australian contract in order to play with the WSC team. West Indian crowds love nothing better than the sight of good fast bowling against quality batsmanship. Rowe, Richards, Fredericks and Lloyd, together with Haynes and Greenidge, promised them the excitement they had not enjoyed from the 1978 Aussies.

In addition to the natural heightened level of interest in the series, the WSC organization mounted a promotional campaign that was unheard of in the Caribbean. By doing this I think they underestimated the seriousness of cricket in the West Indies and the meaning attached to it by the spectators. According to the organizers, the series was going to be something out of the ordinary: Supertests played by superstars – a new dimension in cricket. The people were stirred. And what they actually witnessed was a rather ordinary series plagued by rain. The players themselves must bear some of the responsibility for the crowd's behaviour at some of the games. The many open disagreements with decisions from players on both sides did little to bolster spectator confidence in the umpires. In the heat of competitive cricket at the highest level, it's probably not fair to expect the normal courtesies from a batsman who is given out when he feels that he is not. A little foresight and consideration for others, however, would prevent a batsman from showing disfavour with a decision while he is still in the middle. Of course, when he gets back to the pavilion, he can do as he likes. At least he would not arouse thousands of volatile spectators.

After my marathon spells in Australia, it was decided that I would specialize in the one-day games as I was still not fully fit. Consequently, I played in the fourth Supertest only. I was later to wish that I had been left out from that one, too. On the first day of the game, the crowd stormed the dressing room and I found myself under siege with Rowe and Richards and a couple of the other players. We were trapped in the toilets, bath, and under tables while bottles crashed through the windows and sent glass flying. We all made it to the bathroom and looked through the window where we could see a moat running along the length of the building. We thought that if we could reach it, we could escape the noisy, threatening crowd outside. But the windows were barred by planks embedded in the wall. I can still see Lawrence Rowe banging away at the planks with one of his beloved bats; but the wood never budged. We had pushed the long massage table against the main door in the dressing room; but every shove by the crowd outside inched the door back. Some of us tried to hold the table against the door while ducking the bottles that flew through the window.

After about twenty minutes, that at the time felt like an eternity, the door flew open sending the massage table across the room. We all grabbed bats or whatever else we could get our hands on and waited for the crowd to come in. A frightening few actually entered the room; and, for a couple of seconds, I felt a bit like I imagine the Americans felt at the Alamo. Then we noticed what had saved us. Smoke clouds of tear gas wafted through the pavilion, and we breathed a collective sigh of relief.

Afterwards, a group of us discussed why West Indian supporters would want to attack West Indian players. The Australians had not faced anything like the pressure we had experienced. In fact, they had been whisked off as soon as the trouble started. There appeared to be no reason why the crowd should attack us. After all, not a single ball had been bowled in the match. No action from any of the players could have provoked the crowd. I came to the conclusion that the fact that they were prepared to attack their own players was a sign of a general urge to revolt that the people felt. Their frustrations and anger were not directed at foreigners. They were directed at us. I took this to mean that they were symbolically attacking their political leaders whom they dared not attack in reality. I would hate for the day to come in the West Indies when what I saw in that dressing room became a form of protest on the streets.

On the following Monday, the game started and was played in three days of glorious sunshine unlike the rain that had left the field waterlogged and caused the disturbances on the Friday. The crowd behaviour too was the opposite to what we had seen so recently. It was hard to imagine that among the spectators out there were some of those who had given us the scare of our lives only hours before. Under the circumstances, it would have been impossible for the game to be played out to a decisive conclusion. At least the crowd got to see a couple of good batting displays. Greg Chappell made 113 out of an Australian total of 341 after they had been sent in by Lloyd. He stroked the ball majestically, and never really looked like getting out until he played a lazy cut at an outswinger from King and was caught behind. I managed to get 3 for 60 off 20 overs, including the wickets of Kent for 51 and Marsh for 49 when both of them looked set for big scores.

When we batted, King, Towe, Richards and Fredericks provided the crowd with the kind of batting exhibition which West Indians have grown to expect from their top batsmen. Lloyd, batting at home for the first time in a while, struck 6 fours in 31, while blasting the bowling all over the place. We were finally all out for 476, and in the anti-climactic second innings and Aussies cruised to 117 for 3.

I was to take no further part in Supertest play. In fact, I was not to play World Series Cricket again, apart from the limited overs matches still left to be played. The experiences of that game left a bad taste in my mouth. I must admit that I had been scared out of my wits by the debacle in the dressing room on Black Friday. I had seen unruly crowds before, and had been told tales of disturbances that had taken place previously in the West Indies, India and Pakistan; but it still was not what I had grown up to expect from a cricket game nor from spectators. For the first time since I began to play cricket seriously, I began to think that the game was ugly. It was useless trying to convince myself that it was not really the game that was ugly, but what it could do to the avid supporter under the conditions in which the vast majority of West Indians lived. When any activitity has the meaning for a people that cricket has for the West Indian; when a grown man could cry at the outcome of a game, there is a horror associated with it. Although hard to describe or explain, that horror is quite tangible when it directly affects you. I began to feel that cricket had much to do with that horror. I had to tell myself constantly that the real source of the unpleasant behaviour existed beyond the boundary.

In the limited overs competition, we won eight games, the Aussies two, and two were abandoned because of rain. I played in eight games, bowled 55 overs and took 8 for 222. I suppose that the average of four runs per over was not particularly bad for limited overs games, but it was still above my personal average. I think that it reflected the uneasiness that I felt throughout that troubled series. I was disturbed by what I saw in Barbados and Guyana and at the end of the series I dearly wanted a rest from cricket for a while to try and re-awaken my appetite for the game. I began to feel that I had become, without noticing the transformation, something of a machine. I would turn up at a cricket field somewhere in the world, someone would turn the switch by tossing the ball to me, and I would run in and bowl. I still tried to do my best. I still thought that I had the ball to get the particular batsman out; but cricket had become work in the worst possible meaning of that word. I had consoled myself during the really bad moments of the WSC tour by telling myself that that was precisely what it amounted to. I had chosen a profession and, like most other occupations, it had its ups and downs, and I had to live with them.

Something was lacking in my approach to the game. More

important, it was something that I thought I was fully aware of; but I couldn't quite put my finger on it. I was certainly motivated, and this thing – whatever it was – remained sub-conscious. I felt that something had died somewhere between Guyana and Trinidad and Barbados, and, if I couldn't revive it, there would be little point in continuing to play cricket professionally. When I went to England for the 1979 county season I knew that I had to hunt for the lost feeling that I once had for the game. I hoped that a change of environment would stimulate me enough to find it.

An English summer is not the ideal time for a West Indian trying to regain his lost love for a game that is played at its best in bright sunshine. May 1979 in England was one of the wettest on record. To quell rising despondency and to pass the time while waiting to play, I frequented the pubs around Taunton. I quickly became friends with Chris Greenslade, a publican, and his wife Celia. Chris, with his fat middle and good cheer, was what any doctor would have ordered if he had known the nature of my ailments. I frequented Chris' pub because of the atmosphere he was able to generate there. The lager was good and the people very friendly. Though he has now moved further out of Taunton, most of the Somerset players still visit him often.

On the field, I knew that I had to search within my emotional reserves to find the feeling that I once had for the game. I had an added incentive because the 1979 season would be the first in which I would be playing full-time for Somerset. I came to a decision, after much soul-searching, to try and do my very best, not only for Somerset but in preparation for my return to the official West Indies team. It took a lot of energy; but I had help from good friends, among them Roy Kerslake. Roy, without even knowing it, was the person who was most influential in persuading me to join Somerset. He is a quiet, thoughtful, considerate person whom anyone can trust. He is an ex-player who understands players' feelings better than anyone else I've met. Honest and sincere in his dealings, he is not interested in personal glory but in the welfare of Somerset and Somerset players. He would be an asset to any club. His wife Lynn is of the same mould although she finds it much more difficult to hold back her feelings of frustration about some of the stupidity she sees in the authorities' handling of players' affairs. Later, in appreciation of their friendship and support, expecially at the beginning of that 1979 season when I needed it most, I gave Roy my medal from the 1983 Nat West final! He was, at the time, nursing a broken leg and we had to kidnap him to get him to Lord's to watch the final. He has since left the club.

I was able to conquer the feelings I had started the season with; and I think that Somerset benefited. The team won the Gillette Cup and the John Player League on the final two days of a season that brought the club its first major successes since its foundation in 1875. But I was not alone. Botham batted superbly that summer, as did Viv Richards. Viv blasted 266 runs in four Gillette Cup games. I led the County Championship averages for the club with figures of 393.1 overs, 137 maidens, and 55 wickets for 761 runs: an average of 13.83. In the four games of the Gillette Cup, my 43 overs brought a total of 17 wickets for 92 runs. Included in this was the best return for a final of 6 for 29. In the John Player League, I managed, in thirteen of the sixteen matches to get 16 wickets for 296 in 96 overs. Crickus was not completely absent that season, however. I played in all three of the matches that Somerset lost.

But without a doubt the best experiences of that 1979 summer were the Prudential Cup games in England. The WSC players had been recalled to the official West Indies side, and though there had been some anxiety about how the players who had represented the West Indies in India while we were playing for WSC would react to us, we found those included in our side to be congenial and understanding. While in India, the team, under Kallicharran, had informed the Board that it was opposed to its decision to consider WSC players for World Cup selection; an action which those of us with WSC found childish and aggravating. In the event, when the team gathered in England, Kalli himself, Faoud Bacchus, Larry Gomes and Malcolm Marshall fitted in perfectly with the rest of us. I grew very close to Malcolm, a Barbadian like myself who became my room-mate and was soon to be the fastest bowler in the world. At that time, he was also an accomplished batsman. There are not many cricketers who read the game as well as Macco does. He was fun to be around, and although he did not play a single game in the Prudential Cup he was always cheerful and a source of great inspiration to me.

We retained the Cup by winning two out of the three games we were scheduled to play, one against Sri Lanka having been completely rained off. Our fielding was extraordinarily good throughout the series of one-day games. Lloydie finally managed to mould the group into a professional team of the highest standards with the ex-WSC players forming the nucleus.

The final was my best game of the series. Against England, I took 5 for 38 from 11 overs. All four of the wickets came for only 4 runs from 11 balls, and I was twice on a hat-trick. The fast bowlers on our side were particularly grateful to the England team for their tactics during their innings. Given 287 to win from 60 overs, Brearley and Boycott started the innings as if they were playing in a five-day test. Boycott, mischievous as usual, took seventeen overs to reach double figures; and by the time Brearley was out England needed 158 from 22 overs. I remember Colin Croft telling me, sometime during the course of their stay at the crease, that he hoped that neither of them would get out. By the time they were gone, it would have taken a superhuman effort from batsmen even of the calibre of Gooch and Botham to retrieve the situation.

Our overall performance owed a lot to the batting of Greenidge and, especially in the final, Richards. Greenidge is a totally professional player who approaches every batting situation as if he had made detailed plans. He is a capable, tight player who is not in the habit of giving bowlers a chance to get him out. Richards, on the other hand, almost always provides the better bowlers with a slight opportunity early in his innings. If you fail to capitalize on it he is soon exercising his naturally aggressive instincts and lashing the ball all over the place. Whereas Greenidge methodically picks bowling apart, Richards is much more severe and dashing. I should know how to get both of them out; but because it would give our opponents an advantage and because it is not a foolproof method and I would hate to be responsible for the bowler's average who tried it and failed, I will refrain from suggesting any ideas. It is enough to say that any aggressive batsman hates – yes, really hates – to be restrained for any length of time; and Smokey Richards is no exception.

The West Indies team that went to Australia at the end of 1979 had a good deal to prove. In five previous tours down under (excluding the WSC tours) the West Indians had always been losers and four years previously they'd been totally demolished by the pace attack of Dennis Lillee and Jeff Thomson, and by their own indifferent batting and lack of discipline. The players were still seeking revenge for that defeat. World Series Cricket tournaments had not been blessed with the best of luck. Crickus had slept through mamy of the games, and some other demon had appeared on the scene in the West Indies to confound that tour. Additionally, WSC had brought virtually the same teams together for two seasons in Australia and one in the West Indies, and the results in the Supertests had been absolutely even: in Australia, two victories each and a draw; in the West Indies, one victory each with the other matches drawn in the five Supertests. The games against Bobby Simpson's side could not really be counted because the team had been depleated by defections to WSC and the matches against the WSC Aussies weren't the real thing since neither the Australian nor the West Indies teams were drawn from among the best players. With the settlement between WSC and the International Cricket Conference, test cricket would be test cricket again. During the World Cup, a new feeling of anticipation among most of the world's players could be felt. It was catching.

A summer that had begun in despondency ended with me being chosen as one of the five Wisden cricketers of the year. It was not a bad turnabout. I had succeeded in putting my disappointments behind me. I had stopped blaming cricket for events that were only indirectly to do with the game. I told myself that if I was to continue playing the game, then it would have to be a separate part of my life. I would have to control it and the affects it could have on me instead of it controlling me. I made up my mind to increase the distinction between my self on the field and my self off the field. I did not know until some months later how much this development in attitude was to help me maintain my cool in very highly-pressured situations.

In 1979–80 in Australia, the West Indies finally had their

first authoritative and official triumph over an Australian team. We won two games of the three-game series, much to the pleasure of those nine members of the team who had tasted defeat in 1976. In the period between the two official series, WSC had provided all but six of the team. Furthermore, the WSC nucleus had helped to shape the whole team into a fighting unit that played cricket with a kind of polished ruthlessness that had been foreign to earlier West Indian sides of calypso cricketers. I remember during one test a spectator rudely shouted at one of our batsmen to hit the ball. This senior player shouted back that the beat was no longer calypso, but reggae. 'We've slowed it down a little, man!' he shouted, aware that previous West Indian teams were composed of players with deserved reputations for making a few elegant strokes and then getting out carelessly. WSC changed all that. We became professional in all aspects of the game, including the pacing of it.

In the first test in Brisbane, the Aussies included eight former WSC players, and Greg Chappell was reinstated to lead the team in place of Kim Hughes who was made vice-captain. On our side, Murray, after fifty-two appearances, was chosen to lead for the first time in a test because Lloyd was recovering from a knee operation that some reporters thought would knock him out of the game permanently. Murray won the toss and sent the Australians in to bat, and when Laird and Chappell were in the process of adding 130 for the third wicket, we began to feel that perhaps he had made a mistake. The pitch was extremely good, and in those days there was nothing more disheartening to a West Indian quickie than to have to bowl to one of the Chappell brothers on a good strip. Laird also batted extremely well, and was, I think, unfortunate to be given out, caught behind off a ball that cut away from him. It was one of those things that could have gone either way, and I uttered a silent prayer while the umpire deliberated. I must admit feeling joy tinged with surprise when the decision came in my favour, because Laird had made 92 and, apart from a pretty close lbw decision against Roberts early in his innings, he had looked extremely well set. The Aussies had made 229 for 5 when bad light stopped play. We felt relieved that evening about the score because we knew that the wicket provided us with no help whatsoever.

The Australian bowlers were soon to experience what we felt. After we had bowled them out for **268** – I got **4** for **54** off **22** overs – Greenidge and Haynes added **68** for the first wicket. There is nothing that Viv Richards likes better than a start like that, and he set about the Aussie attack as if he was at home in Antigua on Independence Day. He batted through to lunch on the third day, and was finally out brilliantly caught by my competitive friend Marshie off Lillee for **140** excellently-made runs. The first innings was particularly memorable for me because I got my highest Test match score and enjoyed every minute of it. I was pleased about a last wicket stand of **56** with Colin Croft that established a record for the West Indies against Australia. When I was finally out, I returned to the pavilion with my head high, feeling like the opening batsman I've always felt I could have been had fate not decided differently. We were all out for **441** and, with two days remaining, it appeared that the Australians would have their work cut out to win the game.

McCosker and Laird saw out the third day. On the fourth morning, McCosker and Border fell within the first hour; the latter to an amazing catch that Richards took left-handed at third slip off my bowling. It was one of those chances that I would have been pleased but slightly disappointed had he merely stopped the ball. Australia were **179** for **3** at the time and I thought that we had a more than an even chance of winning. Laird came as close as one could to being bowled off his body from one of Holding's short ones when he had made **10**, and then, trying to evade a bouncer, he lost his helmet which fell inches from the stumps. My friend the sprite was having a field day, for Laird was immediately afterwards given the benefit of the doubt in a run-out decision when he under-estimated King's accuracy from extra cover. That he ended up making **75** in five hours shows how important these near misses can be in terms of the course of a game.

After lunch on that fourth day, Mikey Holding and I held the Australian batsmen in check. I think we bowled something like five consecutive maidens during this period. All the while, the Australians were having the better of the luck. It really hurt when Chappell was dropped by Kallicharran off Holding. It was not until after tea that we could break the **124**-run partnership

when my room-mate Macco Marshall, substituting, held a splendid catch to dismiss Laird off my bowling for 75. By the close
though, Chappell had made 97 and the Australians had consolidated their position.

On the final morning, after he had made 124, Chappell got
out. It took a very good ball from Croft to do the job. That the
odds were firmly against us in this game became clear (and
provided some preview of what awaited us in New Zealand)
when Hookes, first ball, survived an lbw decision that must
have been as close as 'damn it' is to swearing. I'm sure that
Crickus had something to do with the decision in my next over
when I felt that Hookes edged to the wicket-keeper and the
appeal was turned down. By lunch, the Australians had scored
320 for 4 and the game had been saved. They finally and
surprisingly declared in the afternoon after Kim Hughes had
made 130 elegant runs. We lost 3 wickets in making 40 runs;
but there was nothing left in the game by the time Australia
had declared.

We went into the second test at Melbourne with some appre-
hension. A West Indies side had never won a test match at that
ground. Lloydie was back at the helm, though, and we all knew
that with the suggestions buzzing around that he had finally
reached the end of the line he was going to be going all out for
victory. From the very first day, we grabbed the game by the
collar and shook victory out of it. We bowled Australia out for
156. I got 3 for 33 including the valuable wickets of Border and
Chappell. When we batted, we forced 103 for 1 from 18 overs.
Our critics had said that we failed to win the first test because
we did not have a specialist spinner in the side when the wicket
changed to suit that kind of bowling. The selectors continued
with our battery of fast bowlers, and it appeared to pay off. We
accumulated 397 in our turn at the wicket, thanks to a powerful
96 from Richards. We had a lead of 241 when Australia batted,
and no intention of allowing them to repeat their Brisbane
performance. Laird batted well for 69 and Hughes made 70
stylishly; but none of the other batsmen really gave us any
trouble. We bowled them out for 259, whereupon Greenidge
and Haynes undertook the formality of making the few runs
needed to give us a win by ten wickets.

After this game we were pleased with ourselves. We knew

that we had only to draw the third test to become the first West Indies side to have won a series in Australia. Lloydie had silenced those who had considered him over the hill when he made a solid 40 in our first innings. Our fast bowlers had performed consistently well, though I must admit that the wicket did give us some help with its bounce on the first day.

On winning the toss at the beginning of the final test, Chappell sent us in to bat. After Greenidge was out early for 6, Richards and Haynes set about the Australian bowling with such vigour that at lunch the score was 115 for 1; with Richards not out 76 and looking set for a double century. As frequently happens in this remarkable game, between the two intervals there was an almost total reversal of fortunes. Viv was out immediately after lunch, caught behind off a beauty from Lillee. By tea, we had crawled to 166 for 3. After tea, Lloydie showed that he was well and truly back in the saddle by striking a masterful, powerful 121 before he was out in the last over of the day. Early on the second day we were bowled out, mainly by Lillee, for 328.

It seems to me now that it was immediately afterwards that Chappell thrust out his bat at a steeply rising bouncer from Holding and the ball flew straight at me in the gully and Australia were 26 for 3 with both of the Chappell brothers gone. After that, only Border and Laird put up any kind of resistance to Croft and Roberts. The Australians innings closed first thing on the third morning for 203 runs, a much more respectable score than most of us thought they would reach.

Ahead by 125 runs on the first innings, our batsmen set about the Australian bowling as if they were settling a grudge match, which most of them probably thought they were. Richards, Greenidge, Kallicharran, Rowe and Lloyd, all of whom had faced the terror of Lillee and Thomson with trepidation in 1975–6, now batted with assurance, grace and power. When stumps were drawn at the end of the day, we had scored 303 for 4 and were 428 runs ahead. On the morning of the fourth day, there was an impromptu discussion in the dressing room as to when we would declare. A couple of the fellows, remembering some of the indignities they had suffered in this respect during the 1976 tour, advised quite seriously that Lloydie should give the Australians a thousand runs to win. I don't know if Lloyd shared their feelings, but he allowed the innings to run its course; and, when it was finally over three quarters of an hour after lunch, we had given the Australians 573 runs to win. Left with a task of this magnitude, the Australians, tired and dispirited, were quickly bowled out for 165. We had won by the satisfying margin of 408 runs.

The victory party afterwards was one of the happiest I've witnessed as a member of a West Indies side. Those of us who had not been on the previous official tour of Australia knew how the others who had suffered the humiliating defeats four years earlier felt. The jubilation in our camp went past the mere winning of a test match. We had the impression that at long last our cricket had come of age. Greg Chappell had called us the best side in the world after the second test. We had no doubt now that we were.

All that was left for us to do before we returned to the expected acclaim in the West Indies was to go through the formality of a three test tour of New Zealand. We all laughed when we spoke of the New Zealanders. 'New who?' we asked each other. I don't think that there was a member of the team who didn't think that the Kiwi team would be a push-over. Little did we know then that what awaited us in New Zealand was the unpleasant experience of being down under, down under.

7

The jubilation that the members of our team felt when we finally won a test series in Australia was not restricted to the playing field. Because of our experience with WSC cricket, many of us had come to know and like Australia. We had made friends with the Aussie players and enjoyed ourselves after games. I had made good and lasting contacts with some wonderful people. Rudi Webster, the Barbadian fast-bowling doctor who once represented Scotland and Warwickshire was our manager for the WSC series and, after I was introduced to him by Wes Hall, we quickly became close friends.

I soon found that Rudi and I had many interests in common. So close were we that some of my team-mates accused him of favouring the Barbadian contingent of the side in his decisions. Anyone who knows Rudi knows that this is an absurd accusation. As time passed, the other members of the side came to respect and admire the man who, apart from anyone else, provided us with scientific approaches to the game and to the motivational standards of the professional. They found, as I had done, that Rudi was capable of switching from cold analysis to impish practical joke as the occasion demanded. Every year since we first played WSC cricket, the members of the team who happen to be in Australia at the time have spent Christmas at Rudi's house, where everyone is always welcome. Later, when I represented South Australia in the Sheffield Shield, I spent most of my spare time with Rudi and Lyndie. His petite wife Lyndie is a charming, attractive and understanding lady who has that ability, surprisingly rare among cricketers' wives, of being able to accept their husbands' cricketing friends. Lyndie, with the help of some Malaysian ladies, goes out of her way to make the West Indies team feel comfortable during their long periods away from home.

The climate in Australia, the off-field camaraderie with our Australian opponents, friendships built upon during previous tours, and the comfortable feeling we all had in Australia, made the tour a wonderful experience. Probably because of this, we were disappointed at the initial treatment we received when we went to New Zealand. We found the service at the airport and in the hotels poorer than we had become accustomed to in Australia, and even before a ball was bowled most members of the side were disenchanted and just wanted to get the series over and done with.

Of the thirty-four days we spent in New Zealand, we played on twenty-four of them in six different cities, and had three tests thrown in. On pitches and in a climate that proved a little different from Australia's, there was no significant period of adjustment. In spite of the discomfort we felt, we tried to maintain a professional approach. We made up our minds that we would do our best; and we felt that our best would be good enough to beat the New Zealand team.

What we did not take into account was the seemingly never-ending stream of staggering umpiring decisions that plagued us from the very start. Match after match, our efforts were subverted by the men in white coats. Lloyd won the toss for the first test and decided to bat, although no one knew quite how the pitch would play. After Greenidge was out, to the bowling of Hadlee, only Desmond Haynes showed much determination and ability to prevent the ball from striking his pads as we were bowled out for 140. Hadlee had taken five wickets, four of tem lbw, for 34 runs off 20 overs. We did not bat well, and Hadlee had bowled marvellously. Still, we felt that a couple of decisions that went his way could as easily have gone our way.

When New Zealand batted, our fast bowlers took some time to adjust to the difference between the wicket they were bowling on and those they had left behind in Australia. We had become accustomed to bowling a short length on the fast Australian pitches. On the much slower New Zealand wicket, the short ball was not as effective, and the home side, taking advantage of our lack of familiarity with the conditions, mustered 212 runs, mainly through the contributions of Edgar (65) and Hadlee (51).

At close of play on the second day, we had reached 210 for 9.

Desmond Haynes had struck a magnificent century. Hadlee had continued his winning ways and, when we were all out early on the third day with Desmond Haynes being last man out for the second time in the game, the New Zealand pace bowler had taken eleven wickets – six of them lbw.

We had given the New Zealanders only 104 runs to win, but we were by no means defeated. In our team meeting before the start of the New Zealand second innings, we decided that we would attack them by using only the pace bowlers, having tactically considered the conditions we were playing under. We were annoyed at some of the decisions that had gone against us; and Holding, Croft and I decided that we would pull out all the stops and bowl at our best to try to ensure a victory for our side against the odds. Holding had Howarth caught by Greenidge off a very fast ball when the score was 15. Then he clean bowled Wright at 28. I could tell that he was fired up. In spite of the low total that New Zealand had to make, I felt that we now had a real chance, and I think that Mikey must have felt the same way, too. He rushed in and bowled a beauty of an outswinger to Parker who had not yet scored, and the apparently clear-cut edge flew through to Murray who took the catch. To our amazement, umpire Fred Goodall turned down the appeal. Out of pent-up frustration and anger, Holding kicked down two of the stumps at the batsman's end. They say that a photograph is worth a thousand words. Every time I see that photo of Mikey kicking down the stumps, I remember the pent-up frustration we felt throughout the New Zealand tour.

We fought on. After lunch was taken with the home team 33 for 2, Croft cut through the batting. He had Howarth caught at 40 and Coney lbw at 44. It was then my turn. Edgar was caught behind and I produced a fast yorker that got Lees lbw. Ten runs later, the same ball produced the same result with Webb this time the victim. We had them at 54 for 7, and we felt that we had them good, although the two who were responsible for their score reaching 200 in the first innings – Hadlee and Cairns – were at the crease. Then Croft had Cairns caught behind, or so we all thought, but the umpire thought differently. The two batsmen slowly began picking up runs and, unfortunately, Lloydie dropped Cairns when the score was 90. They went to tea with the score at 95 for 8, but even then we felt that we would win the game.

Eight runs later, Parry missed the stumps at the bowler's end while trying to run out Troope and the New Zealanders had beaten the West Indies. Greenidge expressed what we all felt by kicking out a stump. Throughout the match it was clear, at least to us, that the umpires had no intention of giving us the benefit of the doubt, which they constantly did for the New Zealanders.

The umpiring during the second test was, if anything, worse than it had been for the first. We were being no-balled when it was clear that such was not the case. We were having what we considered formality appeals turned down. None of this, however, could account for our atrocious batting in the first innings. After being 190 for 3, we were bowled out for 228, mainly because of suicidal hook shots against the less than lethal bowling of Cairns, who took six wickets.

We struck back on a wicket that proved a little more to our liking. We soon had the New Zealanders reeling at 53 for 3, but their captain, Geoff Howarth, and John Parker, two highly-experienced players, began to pull them around while we shouted ourselves hoarse with appeal after appeal. After Howarth had edged one away-swinger to Murray, Holding shouted so that the umpire could hear 'Man, why you bawling out like that? You'll only get laryngitis.'

At tea Howarth was 99 not out. We were convinced that, whatever we did, we could not win the game. In our opinion, Howarth had been out so many times that we felt it a special injustice that he should make a century. We discussed having umpire Goodall replaced. The players said that we should look into the ways and means of having the match and the tour called off; and many of us were not prepared to go back out on to the field. But we eventually decided that it would not be in the best long-term interests of West Indies cricket to abandon the match and that we should go back out. We finally returned to the field about twelve minutes late after the tea interval. It was not a deliberate protest, although many of us felt not only that it should have been but that it should have been more extreme.

We played purposelessly for the remainder of the day. Howarth reached his century and was 141 not out at close when

New Zealand were 248 for 4. There was a strong body of opinion amongst us that the tour should be abandoned, and we even cleared our dressing room in the event that this should be the case.

The next day, fortunately I think for future test cricket between the West Indies and New Zealand, was a rest day. We had a long team meeting in which the main item on the agenda was the pros and cons of abandoning the series. I think that because it was a rest day we could see things a little more dispassionately, and the idea that it was in the best interests of West Indies cricket to go on, despite what we all considered unfair umpiring, finally prevailed. But most of the members of the side remained bitter.

On the following day, we returned to play cricket only to find that the umpiring had not, in our opinion, improved. Colin Croft, in exasperation, bounced into umpire Goodall in his approach to the wicket. We were forced to apologize to the New Zealand Board and to the umpire for the incident and for Holding's kicking down the stumps at Dunedin. After the incident, we lost all interest in the test. To us, there seemed little point in trying to bowl flat out when you knew that your every appeal would be refused. We went through the motions. Hadlee made a century before Kallicharran bowled him taking a swipe, and the New Zealand innings closed at 460.

We were 232 runs behind with four sessions to go in the match, and our batsmen decided to show the New Zealanders what batting could be like even when they thought that the umpires were against them. Greenidge and Haynes batted like men possessed, reaching 157 without loss and then went on to 225 the following morning before Troope had Greenidge caught at 97. Haynes reached his hundred, as did Rowe and King. The latter with a gigantic six into the open terraces to bring the wretched game to a close at a draw with our score 447 for 5.

By the time we came to the final test, we had resigned ourselves to the negative umpiring. In that last game, the left-handed opener Bruce Edgar scored 127 and on at least six occasions he was extremely fortunate with umpiring decisions, most of them involving catches behind to Murray, including one off Colin Croft when he had been stuck on 99 for half an hour. We played out this match because we had to. I got six wickets in the New Zeland first innings and the game ended in a draw.

The home side was as happy with their success as we were depressed and disappointed – not at having lost but at the way in which we felt that we had lost. Our manager, Willie Rodriguez, refused to show up for the usual end-of-tour press conference; and Lloydie's brief appearance was mainly to emphasize our disappointment with the level of umpiring we had witnessed. By our estimation, at least twelve clear decisions had gone against us during the series. We were happy to be able to put the disaster of playing cricket in New Zealand behind us.

Perhaps the statements that most clearly and accurately sum up the team's feelings about that New Zealand tour are contained in a letter that our captain, Clive Lloyd, sent to the West Indian Cricket Board of Control on our return to the Caribbean after the series. Lloyd wrote:

Dear Mr President,
   The West Indies team had concluded a very heavy travelling schedule and a series of hard-fought cricket matches in Australia and were mentally and physically very tired upon our arrival in New Zealand.

   In New Zealand our reception was quite different and did not bear comparison with our experience during the Australian leg of the tour and, indeed, in all other test-playing countries. In addition, we encountered some very incompetent umpiring.

   In these adverse conditions it is not surprising that we played badly in the first innings of the first test. We made a gallant effort to win the match but from that game onwards under the strain, we were responsible for certain acts of protest which were unprofessional and in retrospect I take the blame for not being firm.

   I realize that these acts of protest against the authority of the umpires were not in the best interest of the game and the conduct thereof.

   I hope it has not seriously tarnished the good name of W.I. cricket which we have built up over half a century.

   For myself and team I wish to offer an apology to the West Indies Cricket Board of Control and the New Zealand Cricket Council through the West Indies Cricket Board of Control.

                                        Clive H. Lloyd

Looking back, I can see how some people could accuse us of behaving childishly on that New Zealand tour; but even an experienced professional can only take so much. When your job is bowling, and you are dependent upon getting batsmen out for a living, when an umpire refuses to give a player out who has clearly struck a ball it is not an easy thing to accept. When we were about to board the plane to leave New Zealand and to leave our depressing experiences behind, Malcolm Marshall turned to me and asked, 'Bird, when are the Kiwis supposed to come to the West Indies?'

I didn't know when they were supposed to tour the Caribbean; but I did know that whenever they did, if any of the fast bowlers in our group were still playing, they would receive an extremely hot welcome.

On my return to Barbados, I felt extremely tired. I had looked forward to swimming at South Point again; but instead found myself sleeping for long hours during the day. I made contact with the local fellows that I had missed while I had been away. For the first couple of weeks I could agree with Willie Rodriguez when he said that we felt alienated and a bit shell-shocked by our experiences in New Zealand. We had all felt that we were playing under different rules than we were accustomed to, and the strain was great. I didn't know how great until I had returned to Barbados and began to relax and try to regain my strength. After a couple of weeks of sleeping and swimming and putting on weight from Gran's cooking, I started to exercise again. The Barbados Cricket Association did not like things as they were and were not happy about me missing the away matches in the Shell Shield competition. I think I rewarded them by taking thirteen wickets in the two games I played.

It was good to be back home, chatting with Gran and the boys from Enterprise, playing dominoes and fishing, getting in a couple of games with the boys in the gap and generally enjoying the splendours of the beautiful island I consider myself lucky to be able to call my home. But all too soon, I was packing my bags and preparing for the West Indies tour of England.

8

On the **27 April 1980** I was stretched out on a BWIA flight headed for London and the beginning of the English tour of five test matches and two Prudential Trophy limited overs games. I felt well rested after my stay in Barbados; but I was not exactly raring to go after my arrival in England. It was cold and damp. It struck me as one of those ironies of life that a country with weather like England's could have been the birthplace of a game like cricket. During that summer, I came to understand why Englishmen constantly talk about the weather: there is so little of it that's good there. It always seemed to be damp or overcast or raining or all three. We won the series by beating England in the Trent Bridge test; but bad weather prevented us from winning by a much wider margin because we were easily the better team.

Interestingly, the first test, the one that decided the series, was the one that England came closest to winning. Although I got seven wickets in the match, it was really Roberts' and Willis' game. Andy took 8 wickets for 129 runs in 49 overs; Willis, 9 for 147 in 46.1. The difference in their impact on the game was that Andy virtually won it with the bat on the cliff-hanger of a last morning.

The English side announced for the test showed a couple of remarkable features: this was the first time that my team-mate from Somerset, Ian Botham, would captain the England side; and the wound in international cricket had been shown to be finally healed with the inclusion of Knott and Woolmer, two WSC players. For our part, injuries to Rowe, King and Croft allowed my room-mate Malcolm Marshall to play his first test in England, as did Bacchus.

As was to be the case for the duration of the series, the weather seriously affected the performances of he two sides and the outcome of the games. Lloyd was forced to leave the field on the first day with the webbing between the first and second fingers of his right hand split when he missed a difficult catch after being obstructed by wicket-keeper Murray (who was to have a trying time). Boycott, Woolmer and Botham escaped chances that enabled England to reach 243 for 7 by the close of the first day. On the second, we bowled them out for the addition of only twenty more runs and, after losing Haynes early, Greenidge and Richards added 88. Afterwards, only Bacchus and Murray – dropped when on 23 – prevented Bob Willis from running through our batting. He finally got both of them; but we had a useful 45-run lead on the third day when we were all out.

Gooch was run out just when he appeared ready to launch into one of his match-winning innings, and then, spectacularly, the rain came. It appeared at one stage that there would be no further play in the game. I know that if the rain had fallen like that in Barbados, we would have packed our bags. Surprisingly, after a much shorter break than anyone expected, we were back in the field to bowl at Boycott and Woolmer who both gave the impression that they were fighting rear-guard actions rather than trying to set up a winning total. By the fourth day, Boycott had batted for more than five hours for his 75 and Woolmer had taken 200 minutes to make 29! As often happens, their slow rate could have affected the batsmen who came after them and England could only muster 252, with seven of their batsmen, including Tavare, Gower and Botham, failing to reach double figures.

We were left with 208 runs to win in just over eight hours. That is, we needed to make 100 runs fewer than we had in the first innings, and in the dressing room we were confident that we would do it easily, even after we lost Gordon Greenidge with the score on 11. Viv Richards then produced one of those batting displays of which only he is capable. He made 48 runs in fifty-six minutes of arrogant aggression before his pal 'Both' produced a beauty of a leg-cutter to have him leg before just before close of play.

On the final morning, with the weather continuing overcast, we needed only 99 runs to win with eight second innings' wickets in hand. Many spectators must have taken our win for granted.

There were very few fans present when Bacchus drove at the first ball of the morning and was caught behind. Willis then bowled excellently to restrain our batting, while Desmond Haynes showed patience and maturity in batting for over five hours for sixty-two runs. He broke down in tears when he was run out after being sent back by Roberts because he thought that he had tossed away our chances of winning the game, although only three runs were by then required. Then Roberts hoisted Botham over long on and we had won by two wickets.

The rest of that series was really a story of rain and more rain and Vivian Richards. He made a wonderful century at Lords, and an unforgettable 65 at Manchester when he took hold of Willis as if the two had a personal vendetta. He scored fifty-three of his runs off Bob, hitting him all over the place until Botham claimed him as his one hundred and fiftieth test wicket. On that tour, Viv scored five centuries: 145 against England at Lords; 131 against Northants at Milton Keynes; 122 against Essex at Chelmsford; 103 against our club, Somerset, at Taunton; 100 even against Glamorgan at Swansea.

The weather also made a mockery of the second test. More than eight hours were lost on the last two days, and this doubtless saved England from going two down in the series. In addition to Viv's hundred, Desmond Haynes also scored a century for us in our only innings of 518 after we had bowled out the Englishmen for 269, 123 of those coming from a resolute and commanding Gooch. It was hard to believe that this was his first test hundred. England's second innings was almost toally rained off, and they finished on 133 for 2. I had the pleasure of having taken both wickets, including that of Gooch, before the rain came.

It was the same old story for the third test: rain. About a third of the game was lost because of it. Andy Roberts was injured at the beginning of the England second innings, and this, together with a stonewall performance by Boycott, made the falling rain almost irrelevant as far as any outcome other than a draw was concerned. Oh, and Clive Lloyd made a blistering 101 in our only innings.

I remember the fourth test particularly well. In the third test I had taken five wickets; and although I was to take another five in this test, I don't remember it for the success as much as

I do for the pain I felt in my right shoulder as I tried to bowl a yorker to Gooch. I had scored 46 in our first innings reply to England's 370, and had joined in an important 64-run eighth wicket stand with Croft. We managed 265, giving England a first innings lead of 105. But then we had them 92 for 9 in their second innings. The single wicket that we needed would have left us 260-odd minutes to score 198 runs. By then, Croft, Lloyd and I were all injured. Willey – who made 100 – and Willis – who refused easy runs and was dropped when the score was 111 – stuck on us and the game was drawn. At the end of that match, we were faced with a depressing list of injuries. I had begun to take pain-killers for the ligament trouble in my shoulder; Rowe was out for the balance of the tour; and Croft, Roberts and Lloyd were also unfit. It didn't help that Collis King, capable at his best of turning a game around in a matter of minutes, was dreadfully out of form.

I might not have played in the fifth test had Croft been fully fit; but I felt that the pain-killers would help. They did; but when their effect wore off the pain I felt when I brought my arm over was excruciating. I was more than a little happy, however, when rain delayed the start until quarter to three on the second day. Then Viv, leading the side in the absence of Lloyd, sent the Englishmen in to bat; thereby giving them the distinction of batting first in all five tests. In less than three and a half hours they were all out for 143. My shoulder held up reasonably well but from time to time during the fourteen overs that I bowled I could feel the pain from my right shoulder down to my elbow. Still, I managed to get 3 for 41.

We started to bat at around seven o'clock that evening, extra time having been arranged because of the morning's loss of play. Half an hour later play had to be abandoned for the night because of the gloom. Seven overs had been bowled and twenty runs scored. We went into the third day 123 runs behind with all our wickets standing. That Saturday was as dark and sullen as an English day could be. In spite of that, Haynes and Green-idge gave us a good start, putting on 83 for the first wicket. Dessie was particularly good, making forty-two runs in what to him must have looked like midnight gloom. Understandably, we were all out for 245 after being 105 for 2. When England batted a second time, Boycott and Gooch survived until bad (or worse) light brought play to a welcome end. My shoulder held up only for an over. When I bowled the fifth ball of that over, it felt as if I had torn my shoulder apart. I wheeled over the last ball and left the proceedings.

No play was possible on the Monday, and with half our bowling attack injured the English side was able to hold on and force what by then had become the inevitable draw. I was named Player of the Series which was some consolation for how my shoulder felt. Some of my friends on both sides had had a good series, in spite of the weather. Botham, in his thirtieth test, became the only Englishman to take 150 wickets and score 1,500 runs in test cricket. Richards had batted well and had led the team with maturity in Lloyd's absence. Malcolm Marshall had shown glimpses of the great all-round player he promised to be. In spite of the physical pain I felt, I was (as the English say) 'chuffed' to receive the Man of the Series award from John Arlott who was covering his last Headingley test. He was a man whose voice I had listened to eagerly and expectantly in Enterprise whilst following the campaigns of past West Indian sides.

9

Because of my injured right arm, I did not play for Somerset after my return from the test series in August. Hugh Gore, my boyhood friend, although also suffering from muscle injuries, put in some useful opening spells of left-arm medium pace. I was happy for his relative success, and for Viv's. He returned after the tour to play two great match-winning Sunday innings.

After the English season was over, I had very little time to rest in Barbados before the team had to tour Pakistan. My arm responded well to treatment and I reported fit for the series which started in November. I learnt from Barbadian ex-test players that Pakistan was not a pleasure cruise. They told me that I would find the food not to my taste, the water undrinkable, and the fans fervent. I later discovered that they were not wrong. Pakistan was not at all to my liking. The series was closely contested, mostly dominated by the bowlers on both sides. We eventually won one-love as we had done in England, and it saddened me a great deal to know that my contribution was poor. I got ten wickets in the tests, much below my best for a series, at about nineteen runs each, much above my average. As in England, the weather had affected almost every test, but Marshall bowled very well, and Richards, of course, was Richards. During the fourth test, after being hit repeatedly by Imran on his left leg, Viv survived to make a dogged 120. In the same game, I took my one hundredth test wicket by bowling Safraz Nawaz. Nearly two days of play were lost to a torrential downpour, and the pitch was so badly covered that it became rain-soaked on the fourth day.

Perhaps the most eventful occurrence of the match, if not the series, had little to do with the cricket itself. On the second day of the game when we had taken to the field, Sylvester Clarke, a fellow-Barbadian, after having been pelted by oranges while fielding on the boundary, suddenly felt he had had enough and hurled a brick into the crowd where it struck a youngster, later identified as the president of the local students' union. The distraught fellow was carried across the field on a stretcher with blood pouring from his head. Play was held up for about twenty minutes while Kallicharran spoke to the crowd entreating them not to riot. Surgeons operated upon the student and, after about two hours, he regained consciousness.

There is no forgiving the spontaneous retaliation of Sylvester Clarke; but what many who commented on his action did not know is that we were the victims of some of the most frightening acts before his loss of temper. I remember once we left a ground in the tour bus on our way to the airport and were met by a crowd of hostile Pakistanis who tried their best to overturn our transportation. They used long poles which they stuck under the chassis and tried to push the bus over. Only quick thinking on the part of our driver saved the day. Those of us who had to field on the boundary were continually pelted with various objects. I was very glad that the student's injury had not been more serious; but I could well understand what made Clarke react the way he did. All in all, after our clean sweep of the three one-day internationals and the sole victory of the four-game test series, we were as happy to fly out of Pakistan as I think most Pakistanis were to see the back of us.

I returned from Pakistan and played in only one Shell Shield game for Barbados before the England tour of the West Indies started. Playing so soon after the rain-affected series in England, the contestants knew each other very well and the series promised to be exciting. Unfortunately, it turned out to be incident-filled, wracked with controversy, and shocked half-way through by the untimely death of one of cricket's most delightful personalities, Ken Barrington.

The tone of the series was established before a ball was bowled on the first day of the first test. The match was to be played in Trinidad and immediately the cancer of insularity that has plagued cricket in the West Indies for so long showed itself. The Trinidadians had been incensed that Larry Gomes, the gifted left-handed middle order batsman, had been omitted from the team that toured England. Now vandals, angry because another

Trinidadian, wicket-keeper Deryck Murray, had been left out of the side, tore up the covers and dug holes in the ground where the bowlers would run up. Consequently, three hours of play were lost on the first day. Our domination of the English team on the field of play was clearly shown, however, by the fact that although this time was lost – and more because of the fickle weather that had haunted us for more than a year – we were still in a position on the final day to claim the last two English wickets off successive balls to win by an innings and 79 runs with the mandatory twenty overs remaining.

Once again, the progress of a game in the West Indies had been affected, at least in part, by the lack of courtesy shown by cricket administrators to the crowd. Although there had been heavy rains the day before the game, and the vandals had left a tap running that further soaked the field, I feel that the crowd could have been prevented from throwing debris into the playing area if someone had used the public address system to tell them exactly why they had been kept waiting for play to start.

Once play was under way, Greenidge and Haynes took advantage of Botham's decision to send us in to bat by making 144 runs off the forty-five overs that were bowled. On the second day, the English bowlers, especially Emburey, managed to restrict us to 365 for 7. After the rest day, Roberts struck a hurricane half century, in the process taking 24 in an over off Botham, and helped us reach 426 for 9 before Lloyd declared.

When England batted, Boycott and Gooch made forty-five untroubled runs off Roberts and Holding; but then Croft, bowling first change on the same wicket where he had taken 8 for 29 against the Pakistanis four years earlier, exploded into the Englishmen's faces. He had Boycott snatched up by Richards at slip, and beat Gooch's bat no fewer than four times in one over. Bowling from the other end, I had the bad luck to clean bowl Gooch with a no-ball. My Somerset captain, Rose, was not quite as lucky. Haynes took him at short leg off bat and pad pushing forward; and at tea England were 97 for 2.

After the interval, Willey was out lbw, and Gomes bowled Downton. All the while, David Gower was batting as though playing in a completely different game and was 47 not out when play ended with England 159 for 7. When he fell lbw in Croft's first over of the next morning, England put up little more resistance. They were all out for 178.

With England 248 runs behind, we asked them to follow on. Two hours were then missed because of rain before Holding, in a wickedly fast spell, got rid of Gooch and Rose, his one hundredth test wicket. At stumps, England were 65 for 2, and their hopes of saving the game depended upon the proven ability of Boycott and Gower. The last morning saw Gower caught behind off Roberts for 27, and Miller provide Croft with his one hundredth test wicket by edging to Greenidge in the slips. At lunch England, at 121 for 4, must have still held high hopes of staving off defeat, mainly because Boycott occupied the crease. At the other end, however, Botham, not content to follow the example his partner showed, lashed out at Richards and was caught by Holding at mid-off. Eight runs later, Holding produced an extremely fast bouncer over Boycott's off stump that he could only fend off to third slip. I finally got back into the game by taking two of the last four wickets to fall, and we had won the first test.

We were happy to be going to Guyana one up in the series. Unfortunately, this happiness was soon stifled by what came to be called the Jackman Affair. The rain fell in Guyana incessantly for about a week, cancelling the Guyana–England game, and we waited in our hotel rooms while attempts to stage limited overs games also had to be set aside because of the downpour. Other storm clouds were gathering. England's vice-captain, Bob Willis, had developed knee problems early in the tour and it became clear that he would be unable to complete the series. He was replaced by Robin Jackman, the Surrey bowler, who the Guyana government immediately announced would not be allowed to play there because of his contacts with South Africa. The second test was cancelled in an atmosphere of international political and sporting controversy.

I couldn't see what all the fuss was about. I myself would not play cricket in south Africa under the circumstances that presently exist there; but I have nothing against playing against those who do not share my point of view. I thought that the Guyanese government had gone too far, but they are entitled to make whatever decisions they want. I hoped that some way to continue the series would be found during the five days that

I waited anxiously in Enterprise as the politicians from the four other islands where tests were scheduled to be played met in Barbados to discuss the situation.

After the decision to continue the series was announced, the two teams had to recover the momentum that had been lost in the meantime. England played a one-day game against Barbados, which we lost by eleven runs. I took 2 for 38 in my 10 overs; but it was clear to me that a year of non-stop cricket at the highest level had begun to take its toll. The break for the deliberations on the Jackman Affair seemed not to have provided enough rest, and I therefore opted out of playing in the Barbados–England four-day game. Once again, I was criticized by reporters for a reluctance to represent my island. It hurt; but I felt that I had to do what was best for myself.

I tried to raise my spirits for the Barbados test. Kensington Oval was packed on the first morning, not only with the locals who had come to see their heroes perform but by about 2,000 English tourists who had taken special package tours to fit in the test match. The pitch was greener and had more grass on it than I had ever seen before on a Kensington wicket. I began to feel good. I've often thought that in the West Indies, with a team that includes four and sometimes five fast bowlers, the wickets are too lifeless. That would never happen in Australia or England; and it would be like finding a green top in India or Pakistan.

Botham won the toss and put us in to bat, and his tactic appeared to have paid off when at lunch we were 72 for 4, with Richards, whom the majority of the crowd had come to see bat, back in the pavilion after only facing two balls, gleefully caught by his mate Botham. Jackman, the cause of the cancellation of the second test, was now the cause of more discomfort for us. He had taken the wickets of Greenidge and Haynes.

Enter Lady Luck. This time she waved her wand over Larry Gomes who was bowled by a no-ball from Dilley when on 7, then dropped at 14 and 38, and finally mis-stumped at 49, all off the despairing Emburey. But he stayed with Lloyd while 154 runs were added. The wicket was green, the ball moving about, and four of our top batsmen were out, so I have to count the even hundred that Lloydie made among the best innings I have seen him play. He pounced on anything loose and dispatched it with maximum force to the boundary. After he was out, caught at square leg off Jackman, Gomes soon followed, also caught, but this time by Botham in the slips off Dilley. He had batted for four hours when, without luck, he would hardly have survived fifteen minutes. Mainly because of the partnership between Lloyd and Gomes we reached 265, many more than we had expected earlier in the day.

Probably because we had not expected to make so many runs, the fast bowlers considered the 265 we did make to be adequate. Fired up and aggressive, Holding began the England innings with an over of fearsome pace to Boycott. Five balls flew quickly towards his throat before the sixth ripped his off stump from the ground with Boycott standing steady as a rock. Roberts followed by having Gatting caught in the slips, and I got my second delivery past Gooch. David Gower faced the music for about an hour while scoring 17 before he fell to Croft.

Roland Butcher, the Barbadian who had been picked to play his first test for England, stayed around for a while before he fell in much the same way as had Gower. England were 72 for 5, and reeling. In situations like this, England can normally depend upon Ian Botham. There's nothing that motivates Ian like a challenge. In this respect, he is very much like his buddy, Viv Richards. But we on the West Indies team have played against Ian on many occasions and we know what he's capable of when he gets going. Lloyd called Holding back for a second spell, and Mikey produced an over every bit as fast and furious as the one he had given Boycott. After being dropped by the wicket-keeper, Botham snicked the fourth ball again, this time with a different result. The last ball of the over took Bairstow's wicket, and England were all out for 122.

In the fifteen minutes of play remaining at the end of the second day Greenidge was lbw for a duck and Croft was sent in as night-watchman. Since his 53 in England in the first test of the 1980 series, Greenidge had had a run of low scores. I thought that he was going through a bad patch, but others felt that his batting was suffering because of the ill-will that had been stirred up after the publication of his biography during the English tour. In his book he had said some things about his team-mates that hurt, and for a while there was a great deal of discomfort in the dressing room because of this. Many of us felt that Gordon was having problems that had little to do with us. Raised in England, he appeared to think that he was not accepted in the West Indies by West Indian crowds. But we knew him to be a professional, and expected at any time that the string of low scores would come to an end. More recently, Gordon has changed. He has become more mellow and is still capable of making the very best fast bowling look totally ordinary.

A shadow fell over the proceedings on the third day. Before play began, players and officials stood for a minute's silent tribute to Ken Barrington, England's assistant manager and a great opening batsman in his day, who had died suddenly of a heart attack in his hotel room the night before. The English team appeared shattered at his loss. For the rest of the tour the players sauntered around as if they couldn't wait to get it all over with. The title of the book an English writer produced about the series is very apt: *Another Bloody Day in Paradise*.

Viv Richards, having been out for nought in the first innings, proceeded in the second to take full advantage of the English bowling by scoring 100 with a four off the second ball of the final over. He had batted with Haynes, Mattis and Gomes; but it was his innings that lit whatever spark there was on that gloomy Sunday.

We went into the rest day 388 runs ahead; but Lloydie decided to bat on until lunch on the fourth day. In that time, Richards extended his score to 182 not out and with Lloyd added 153 for the sixth wicket. The skipper contributed 66 well-made runs before he fell lbw to Botham; and later declared at 379 for 7.

England faced a mammoth 523 to win, which would have been an ordeal even in happier circumstances. And if they thought that they could stone-wall, Holding had other ideas. He produced an over equal in ferocity to his first in the previous innings. The fifth ball struck snake-like at Boycott's collar, hit a defensive glove, and lobbed gently to me at gully. The sixth simply flew past Gatting's bat and into the leg stump. Gooch and Gower weathered the storm and produced batting of great application to add 120 runs. We were never worried, and when Gower played an uncharacteristic stroke to a Richards delivery that bowled him, we knew that the end was in sight. Roland Butcher gave himself all sorts of anxiety in scoring 2 in twenty-five minutes and Botham appeared to be somewhere else when he hung his bat out to a Roberts outswinger and was caught at slip. Only Gooch of the English batsmen appeared to be able to handle the conditions. He seemed unmoved by what was going on at the other end, and had reached 88 out of 166 for 5 at close. He reached his second test century on the last day, and for an hour he and Willey proved more difficult to get out than we had thought possible. Croft got the benefit of the doubt in an lbw decision against Willey, had Bairstow caught behind in the same over, and then bowled an outswinger that Gooch hit low and hard to my right at gully. I then clean bowled the two tail-enders and the morose third test was over. I think that the English players were relieved.

The rest of the series was comparatively quiet. Neither of the teams could have taken much more tension, and the weather gratefully allowed England to escape a clean sweep as the last two tests were drawn. Richards and Willey made centuries for their respective teams in the fourth test in Antigua, with Richards' performance being lauded by his countrymen with ovations second only to those they had earlier given him at his wedding. Gooch made 150 in Jamaica to add to his century at Kensington, and showed his team-mates that our fast bowling was not completely unplayable. He also made 83 in Antigua. The only comforts England could have had from that tragic series were the performances of Gooch and Gower, two great strikers of the ball who would be assets to any cricket team. I had cold comfort from the series. It was not one of my best. I got only ten wickets for an average of over thirty. Playing cricket non-stop for a few years had now taken its toll. I was beginning to struggle to stay fit, and the stop–start progress of the series did not help. I began to wonder how long I could keep the pace up. The Bird's wings were a little clipped, having been some thirty pounds lighter after my trip to Pakistan.

10

Not for the first time in my career, I felt wretched about cricket when I left Barbados for England to play for Somerset in the summer of 1981. I was dissatisfied with my overall performance in the series against England at home, and it was of little consolation to blame this on the pain I had felt, from time to time, when I bowled. The whole series, it seemed to me, had been played as if under a dark cloud. Although we had won, the cricket was not really enjoyable. I tried to forget the miserable experience by telling myself that we were paid to win, we had won, and that was that.

The summer in England was vastly different. My shoulder did not give me as much trouble as it had in the West Indies and, for once, the sun shone for most of Somerset's games. I contributed, significantly I think, to the club's superb performance that year. We won the Benson and Hedges Cup, and I took 5 for 14 from 11 overs in the final against Surrey. We were runners-up in the John Player Sunday League, and finished third in the county championship, in which I claimed 87 wickets at fifteen runs apiece. Botham and Richards also had great seasons for the club; and, by the end of the summer, we were all flying high.

It seemed like just a couple of days before I found myself once again packing my bags to go to Australia for the three test series beginning in November. By then, I had truly come to like Australia and the Australians, and looked forward to the trip.

The 1981–2 series in Australia was hard fought; and perhaps deservedly drawn. The Australians played extremely well; but, for the first time in a very long while, our side began to show serious chinks in its armour. That we were not invincible became clear during the very first test. Greg Chappell won the toss and chose to bat first on the same Melbourne Cricket Ground wicket where Australia had lost to Pakistan less than two weeks earlier. It appeared a very bad decision when Holding took two wickets in the fifth over of the innings. Laird and Chappell were his victims; and very soon afterwards Wood fell in the same way – caught behind – but this time off the bowling of Roberts. Australia were in a lot of trouble at 8 for 3. Border quickly followed with the score at 26, again caught behind off Holding, who was bowling very quickly and getting the ball to move about. Kim Hughes then batted extremely well to make 100 not out. He was dropped twice at 66 and 76 but these chances did not detract from an innings of class and courage. When the last wicket, Alderman's, fell at 198, Hughes looked as though he could have gone on at least until close of play, about three quarters of an hour away.

We found ourselves immediately in trouble against Lillee. After Bacchus, opening in place of Greenidge who was injured, was dismissed off Alderman's third ball to an excellent slip catch by Wood, this supreme fast bowler produced wonderful deliveries to remove Des Haynes and Croft, sent in as night-watchman. Then we had the shock of our lives when Richards edged a very quick one into his stumps off the last ball of the day. We were 10 for 4, and to the 40,000 screaming spectators beginning to look like very ordinary mortals playing a test match against a good bowling side.

For most of the morning on the second day, Lloyd and Gomes tried their best to retrieve the situation. Gomes was lucky to survive a chance in the slips off Lillee; but Lloyd went first, mistiming an on-drive off Yardley. The batting was then left up to Gomes, Dujon (playing in his first test), and Murray. After them would come the three fast bowlers. Dujon batted exceptionally well, trying to blast us out of the disastrous situation into which we had fallen. He was out trying to hook Lillee out of the ground. Gomes followed quickly afterwards snicking a catch to first slip. With this wicket, Lillee passed Lance Gibbs' test match record of 309 victims, a deserved achievement for a fast bowler of unusual stamina and ability. The rain came as if to bless the accomplishment, while the crowd cheered and the public address system played one of many Aussie songs.

The next day, I made seven runs that enabled us to edge past the Aussie score. We were all out for 201. Lillee had taken 7 for 87, his best figures in a test, and the game was evenly balanced. Wood was dropped by our usually safe skipper in Holding's second over, and the opening pair added 82 important runs before I got Wood to edge one behind. Laird batted well for 64 before Croft unsettled and then dismissed him with a perfect yorker that struck him dead in front. Holding came back for his second spell off a short run and moved the ball sufficiently to baffle the Aussies and take three wickets, including that of Hughes, clean bowled for 8. When I got a yorker under Yardley's bat towards the end of the day, Australia were 217 for 7, only 214 ahead. We returned to our hotel that evening confident that victory would be ours.

That confidence seemed justified the following morning when the Australians could add only five more runs, three of them extras, while Holding collecting the last three wickets, earning himself the distinction of becoming the first West Indian bowler to get eleven Australian wickets in a test. Murray also broke a record: he took nine catches in the match.

A sudden change in our fortunes and in the game came when, with the score at 4, Bacchus was leg before to Alderman and Viv missed the second ball he faced and was clean bowled for a duck. We never recovered. Only Dujon showed any defiance, recovering after he was bowled by Lawson when 27 off a no-ball to bat for more than two hours trying to stem the tide. We were bowled out for 161 and the test was lost early on the final day.

It had been a good match that, until our second innings, could have gone either way. Richards had been clearly out of form. What we found disturbing was that in the flow of the game chances that would normally have gone our way had gone against us. But there was no doubt in our minds that the Australians were a very good team indeed, and if we were not careful, we would lose the first test series since I had become a member of the side in 1977 (if you exclude the forgettable tour of New Zealand).

The second test was drawn. One of the things I remember about it was that the Australian second innings was the first time for a long while in a test that I had failed to gain a single wicket in an innings. We gave the Australians 373 to win; but the overcast conditions and the resultant loss of playing time made it nearly impossible for us to bowl them out. A good, determined innings by Dyson, who made 127 not out, was an additional major obstacle to our success.

Before the third test at the end of January 1982, our side faced the prospect of defeat in a series. Our loss at Melbourne was only the second we had experienced in seventeen tests since the end of WSC in 1979. All the members of the team knew that a second defeat – or even a draw – would be humiliating. We also knew that our star batsman, Viv Richards, needed a good knock to regain his form, and Holding, in spite of his eleven wickets in the first test was injured, as was Greenidge. Haynes and Bacchus were finding runs extremely hard to come by; and I was, quite simply, not producing the goods. A lot would depend upon Lloyd, Gomes and our new find Dujon if the Frank Worrell Trophy was not to slip from our grasp.

Lloyd won the toss and sent the Australians in to bat on a pitch that looked as if it would have some early life. Roberts soon had Laird caught down the leg side by Dujon, wicket-keeping in place of David Murray who had broken a finger. With the score at 8, Wood attempted a cut off the same bowler and I managed to grab the chance in the gully at the second try. Dyson then went in the same fashion as Laird off Holding's bowling. Hughes on 17 failed to get into position because his toe had been badly struck by one of Mikey's yorkers, and in attempting to force the same bowler only succeeded in edging hard to Greenidge at second slip, Chappell batted with more luck than skill but managed to add more than a hundred runs with Border before he was caught off Holding to dismiss him just after tea. The Australians were then 122 for 5. Chappell had batted for most of the day with what must have been an extremely painful left hand because he was repeatedly struck on the glove. My friend Marsh then, as is his style, lashed out aggressively in scoring 37 in one hour, before he hooked at a Croft bouncer and was cruelly struck on the side of his face. He wanted to remain on the field, and actually faced another over before good sense got the better of courage and he retired hurt. Marsh is among the gutsiest cricketers I've met. He's never afraid to take the fight to the opponent, and is always looking for a way to get the upper hand. Off the field, he's as warm and charitable as he is competitive and stern on it. Yardley replaced Marsh only to be yorked by Croft when he appeared to be expecting a short one. Australia ended that first day on 204 for 6. Border, solid and correct, was 78 not out and looked set for a certain hundred.

The next day, they added only a further thirty-four runs while losing the rest of their wickets. Marsh returned but quickly edged a catch to the keeper. Border was well caught, again by Dujon, without adding to his overnight score. Roberts bowled Lillee all over the place and Holding yorked Pascoe. I had bowled seventeen overs without getting a wicket; but Australia's score did not look hard to get past.

Chappell and Hughes, the captain and vice-captain of the Australian side, were both injured while batting and did not take the field when we started our second innings. Lillee then pulled up halfway through his fifth over. But the Aussie spirit was clearly evident as, with three of their key players off the field, they still managed to reduce us to 92 for 4 before tea. Greenidge was gone, as was Haynes, off Thomson's bowling. Bacchus and Richards left in successive overs. Lloyd and Gomes, in one of the many left-handed partnerships they were to play for the West Indies, then steadied the ship by putting on 102 runs. Both of them had chances at low scores, but on the whole batted sensibly until Lloyd was out just before the close.

On the third day, Gomes steadily progressed to his century with help from Dujon and an admirably steady Roberts. By the time I was out, Gomes was left on 124 not out, and we had built a healthy first innings lead of 151. It seemed impregnable when Wood was smartly caught and bowled by Holding at 10 and twenty-five runs later Dyson edged an outswinger to first slip. But Laird and Border, coming in ahead of the injured Chappell and Hughes, batted well on the excellent pitch to take the score to 100 by the close. At lunch on the third day Laird was 71, Border 74; Australia were 172 for 2 and the game was slipping away from us. Then Laird edged Croft behind and was out for 78. Border was at the time 95 and the two of them had added 166 runs. Border, obviously enjoying batting on the good strip, made his hundred with Hughes (using Dyson as his runner) supporting him at the other end. It took an outstanding catch by Dujon off Roberts just after tea to dismiss Border whose 126 appeared to have saved the day for Australia and given them the Frank Worrell Trophy. This seemed especially so as the two from the infirmary, Hughes and Marsh, batted through the rest of the day.

Australia began the final day 341 for 4, a lead of 190, and must have thought that they had won the series since they only needed a draw to do so. I had only taken a single wicket in the game by that time and was bone tired on the fourth day.

The night before the last day, a team meeting was called by the skipper and the general feeling expressed by him was that we were not putting enough into the bowling effort. I for one thought that this was an unfair assessment. I considered that credit should be given where it was due. The Aussies played extremely well, even outplaying us in the batting department. You have to expect people to do well at times, and they took the job to heart.

On the morning of play, Roberts and Holding started off, but Roberts had only bowled one over when the skipper decided to bring me on upwind as a change of tactics.

First Marsh drove a fierce catch to Haynes who took it nicely, providing Mikey with yet another wicket. Then Hughes turned one of my short ones to the right of Bacchus at leg slip. The fielder dived spectacularly and came up with the ball. I was overjoyed. The success gave us the push we needed to go flat out. Mikey bowled a very fast off-cutter that found Chappell plumb in front and not offering a shot. My efforts were rewarded when Yardley was bowled by a fast inswinger I tried after giving him two going away. Bacchus repeated his feat against Hughes by taking Thomson, and Lillee was caught behind. We had the breakthrough that we so badly needed. In under an hour, Australia had lost six wickets for twenty-four runs. I had taken 4 of them for 5 runs from 20 deliveries. Lloydie had said the night before that we could win and would be looking at something like 250 runs to win if the wicket behaved as it had done during the last few days. In the event, we took some blinders, the most incredible being that taken by Bacchus to dismiss Kim Hughes, and we were left with exactly 238 to win.

In our dressing room we felt that we would be able to make the runs if we continued to play the sensible game that we are

I've never minded helping out an autograph hunter.

The West Indies touring team, 1984. *Back row* (left to right)
A. L. Logie, E. A. E. Baptiste, P. J. Dujon, D. L. Haynes,
R. A. Harper, C. A. Walsh, M. A. Small, M. D. Marshall,
R. B. Richardson, T. R. O. Payne, D. J. M. Waight (Physiotherapist).
Front row (left to right) W. E. St John (Assistant Manager),
M. A. Holding, I. V. A. Richards, C. H. Lloyd (Captain),
J. L. Hendricks (Manager), C. G. Greenidge, H. A. Gomes,
J. Garner.

Keeping the skipper in trim.

Bowling to Allan Lamb in the First Test versus England at Birmingham, 1984.

Stooping to conquer – in the slips with Gordon Greenidge in the Third Test at Leeds, 1984.

Action from the West Indies' tour of Australia in 1984–85 (*and opposite above*)

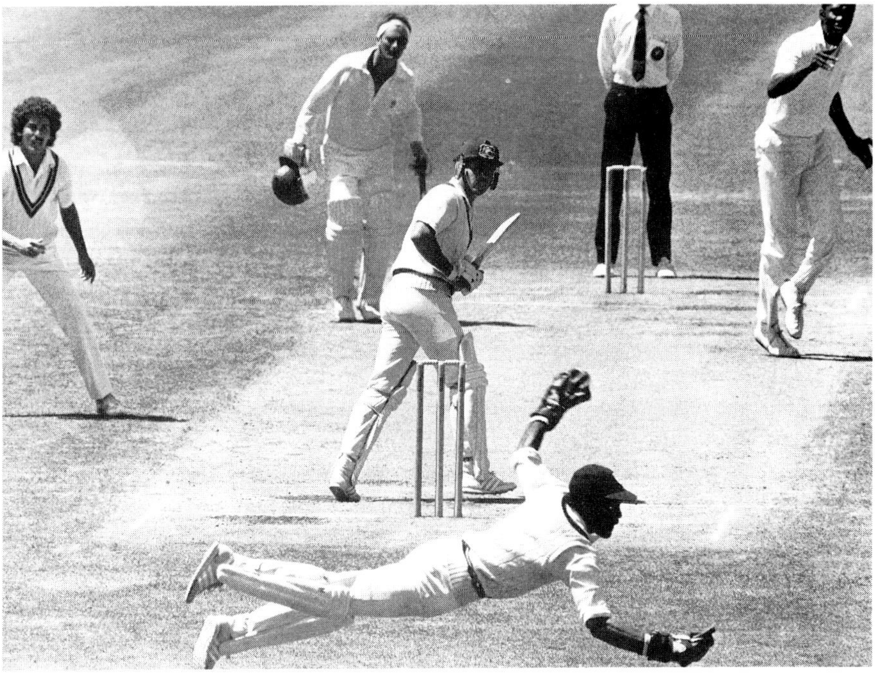

My 200th Test wicket, taken in the Second Test against
Australia, 1984.

My wife Heather and daughter Jewel.

Leaning against the newly renovated house in which I now live.

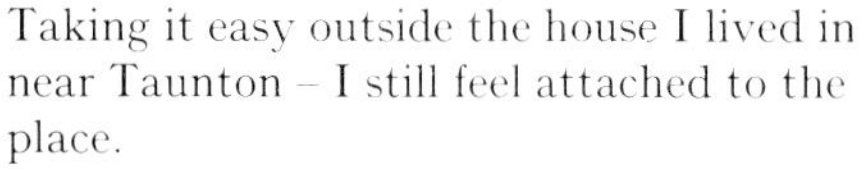

Taking it easy outside the house I lived in near Taunton – I still feel attached to the place.

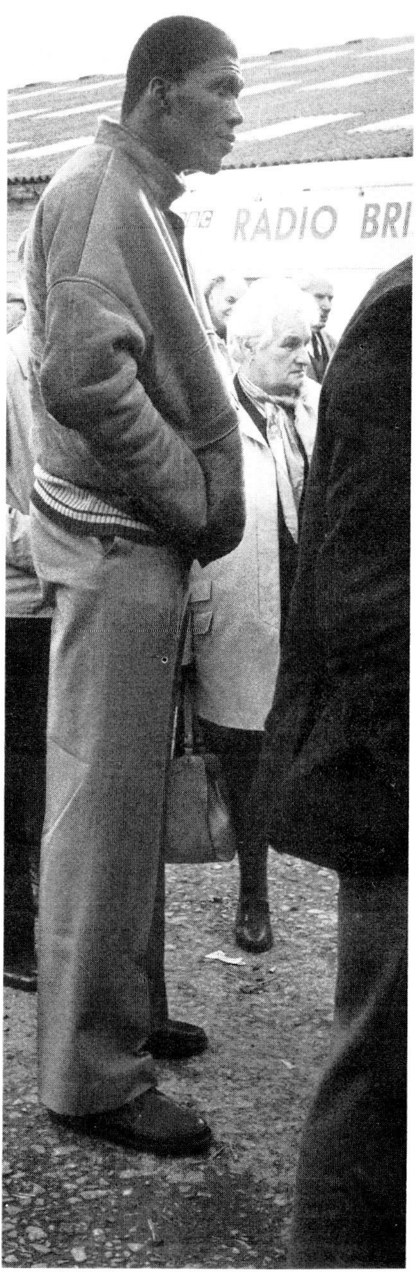

At the public meeting of Somerset rebels in Shepton Mallet, November 1986.

Sitting at home in Barbados with my grandmother Editha.

used to and also the wicket was still playing easily. The batsmen agreed that, in Lillee's absence, the danger man could be the off-spinner Yardley. We were going to go for it, and that meant that someone would have to go for him.

We then settled back to watch, and suffer a little setback when Haynes got a demon from Thomson and could only edge it to the keeper. Greenidge escaped a confident appeal for caught behind off Thomson and Marsh, acting as captain, brought on Yardley after eight overs with our score at 39 for one.

We knew that this was the make or break stage of the game. Richards had been out of form, but he had made 42 in the first innings and at times had looked like the Viv we knew. Greenidge was not fully fit and his batting suffered as a consequence. In six overs, they took forty-three runs off Yardley including a Greenidge swept six that would have broken the heart of any bowler. They did have their share of the luck, Marsh missed a stumping chance against Richards when he was on 32, but we had succeeded in carrying out our plan when Yardley was taken off the bowling. Richards and Greenidge put on 100 runs before they both got out in quick succession. Marshie pulled off an acrobatic catch to get rid of Greenidge for 52, and Richards was bowled by a good one from Pascoe. We were back to the solid combination of Gomes and Lloyd to see us through. They batted steadily to tea when the score was 121 for 3, 115 runs away from victory. The Australians let a very important chance go begging when an edge from Lloyd flew between Marsh and Border in the slips. We were 143 at the time, and the game might have had a very different outcome had that chance been held.

At the beginning of the mandatory twenty overs we were still some seventy-odd runs away from our goal. Lillee came back in spite of injury and, bowling off a shortened run, conceded seventeen runs in four overs before he gave up. Pascoe gave us an anxious moment when he bowled Gomes with sixty runs yet to be scored. We were aware of how the Australian tail had folded and doubtless they had similar thoughts when Bacchus appeared not to have the steadiness of nerve that the occasion demanded. But Crickus was definitely on our side. Bacchus drove Yardly straight at Pascoe and was dropped at 187 for 4. Lloyd pulled Yardley just in front of Malone at 198; and then

Yardley showed that he could be the sinner as well as the sinned-against by dropping the skipper off Thomson.

When the scores were level, Bacchus finally succumbed, hooking at Pascoe, and Dujon played out the over to give Lloyd the satisfaction of making the winning runs on what we all thought at that time would be his last test appearance in Australia. When Lloydie drove Thomson for the winning runs, Holding, Croft and I rushed on to the field and chaired him off. We were delighted. We had won the game, drawn the series, and kept the highly-prized Frank Worrell Trophy.

In addition to the tests, the series was a highly successful one for us. We won the Benson and Hedges World Series Cup for limited overs competition after losing two of our first three matches in the preliminary rounds. We then had seven consecutive victories to qualify for the best of five Grand Final where we beat Australia 3–1. Personally, I had only really reached my best on that last day of the last test. I was so tired from having played so much cricket over the previous years but it didn't stop me taking advantage of the luscious hospitality Rudi Webster and his wife offered while we were in Australia. Others took a rather different view of my performance, however, and for the 1982 season I was contracted to play for South Australia in the Sheffield Shield competition. I flew halfway around the world to Barbados, Enterprise, Gran and the boys in the gap and had a much-needed rest.

11

On returning to Barbados after our tour to Australia, we were approached by members of the selection committee enquiring about the availability of players for the forthcoming Shell Shield series. These approaches were made in the form of requests for players to participate in trial games. Can you imagine the stupidity of asking Test players who had just gone through a gruelling three months to turn up at trials when the days could have been spent relaxing and building up their mental and physical resources.

During the Australian tour I was one of several team members playing with injuries, my knee having started to act up. Why should I turn up at a trial game?

The other irritating part of this game is that the majority of people in charge are only interested in how many people come through the turnstiles, and are not all genuinely interested in the players' fitness. I played the last two games for Barbados and returned to England.

Before I had bowled a ball for Somerset that year I had to have my cartilages removed.

I had a rather indifferent English season for Somerset in 1982, mainly because I was plagued by a knee injury that had first affected me during the Australian series. I recovered enough, I thought, to take up my contract with South Australia towards the end of the year. During my previous visits to Australia I had come to love the country and its people and I felt that I would be accepted there easily. I was not disappointed.

In Adelaide I lived in Glenelg and also played for the local side. Hilditch, Haysman and Johnson also played for both South Australia and Glenelg. I loved the little city with its neat holiday beach areas about seven kilometres from Adelaide. I lived alone in a two-bedroom flat over the city's main shopping plaza, but was still within two minutes walk of the beach. It was like Enterprise. I spent most of my afternoons, when I was not playing cricket or doing promotional work for the firm that employed me, lazing on the beaches.

The only disappointment that I had during my first season with South Australia concerned money. My contract had stipulated that I would be paid a certain sum and released if necessary to play for the West Indies. The manager who signed on behalf of the firm left the company soon after I left Adelaide to play for the West Indies against the Indian touring team, and it took about six weeks for me to get my salary. When I did get paid, the money was short. There was also an undertaking to pay my taxes, and to this day I am still owed about eight thousand US dollars. I know that I am considered something of a militant as far as financial negotiations are concerned; but it is only because I know that fast bowling is a hard job that takes a heavy physical toll and that I won't be able to do it forever. I need to save now for the day when my right arm doesn't come over quite as fluidly as it should.

There were also some rumours that I had taken Glenelg for a ride because of the recurrent injuries I suffered during my first season. I can honestly say that I have never taken money under false pretences, and that I don't intend to. If I am not fit, I am not going to play cricket. I know that the spectators have come to expect certain standards of performance from me and I'm expected to maintain those standards over the entire playing period. Sometimes I think that those connected with cricket think that the players are infallible. Perhaps the rumours were started by those who attempted to use me and was their way of getting back at me when I refused to be manipulated.

I enjoyed the friendship of the South Australian players. Steve Wunke, David Johnson, Mike Hayesman and David Hookes were always jovial. We enjoyed each other's company and spent a great deal of free time checking out the pubs together. Andy Hilditch, although a lot quieter than the rest of us, was a lot of fun in his way; and Brian Vincent was our champion entertainer. They made playing and living in South Australia thoroughly pleasant. I felt at home, away from home.

Howard Mutton, our manager, was a great help to me and did everything possible to make me comfortable in my new surroundings. His wife invited me to their home on numerous occasions to have dinner with the family. A retired school master, Howard was steady and consoling, his only criticism of me was that he was unable to see me in the nets. He was always great fun to be around. Richard Watson, the club's secretary, was also very pleasant and friendly, as was Rob, another club secretary. In all, I found the SACA staff very helpful and always courteous in their dealings with me. Michael Mason and Chris, two physiotherapists, got to know me well because of my different stresses and strains and always wanted to engage me in conversation about Barbados and the West Indies.

Perhaps the most influential person I met during my stay in Adelaide was John Inverarity. He was 'Dad' until I turned thirty, and then 'Uncle John' because my grey hair was beginning to show and it got embarrassing for him. A very quiet gentleman with whom I spent many evenings visiting his family, he was always willing to lend advice and help. Though forty years old, he still got in line wonderfully and experienced the same thrill playing against Michael Holding that he had when facing Wes Hall twenty years earlier. I think that his coaching improved my batting enormously.

When I got to South Australia, everyone warned me that Rodney Hogg was the most difficult person in the world to get along with. I didn't find that to be the case. Rodney is ruthlessly frank and honest; and always looking to stir things up a bit. I was shocked to discover that he had an extremely low opinion of his talents. After about three months of steady conversation concerning self-confidence and motivation, I think that I was able to help him change his self-perception.

The Glenfell Tavern sponsored the South Australia cricket team and was where you could find the players any day that it was open. Among my regular team-mates, Chris Harms, Glen Bishop, Bob Zadow and Kevin Wright could always be expected to be bending an arm and an ear. Wayne Philips was away on tour for a few games; but then he started playing for SA regularly and proved to be great fun. Jeff and Ron, who managed the Tavern, were great characters and witty conversationalists. I have to thank all of these people and many others too numerous to mention for making my stay in Adelaide so wonderful.

In spite of my injuries I worked hard for South Australia;

and I enjoyed it among such a good bunch of friends.

I returned to Barbados at the beginning of 1983 so I would be available for selection for the test series against the touring Indians. But on arrival I was confronted by an irritating situation. The West Indies Cricket Board of Control, no doubt under pressure from the sponsors of the matches, had stipulated that cricketers must represent their countries in at least one Shell Shield match before the start of the tests against the Indians in order to be eligible for selection in the tests. Although I had a letter from my Australian doctor saying that because of bursitis in my right shoulder I should not bowl for two weeks, after missing the Shield games entirely I anxiously awaited the test team's selection.

During that time, I thought how stupid the Board's stipulation was. I could understand their concern that the absence of test players from the Shield competition affected its ability to draw spectators; but the authorities implied that the players were unwilling to represent their countries after they had reached test level. Nothing could be further from the truth. If fit and available, all the players see it as an honour to play for our countries and a privilege to give back something to the local game which has given us so much.

Controversy arose again over the selection of Larry Gomes and myself because we did not play any Shell Shield games. We were selected on our past performances and only because the captain had stood up for us. It is ironical that though you are playing the second highest level of cricket you still have to qualify when your performances have shown that you have been keeping active.

I was relieved to be chosen for the first test; but, in retrospect, perhaps I shouldn't have been. The series against the Indians was a disappointing one for me. It soon became clear that my shoulder was going to give me much more trouble than I had anticipated. We won the first test in Jamaica, thanks mainly to some fine bowling from Roberts in the Indian second innings when he took 5 for 39 and cleaned them up for 174 after our batting could only manage 254 in reply to the Indians' first innings of 251. By tea on the last day the match seemed to be heading for a tame draw until Viv Richards blasted 61 runs off thirty-five deliveries. Then Dujon lifted a full toss over square leg off the second ball of the last possible over of the game to give us victory by four wickets. I had taken 2 for 41 in the first innings and 0 for 16 in the second.

The Indians drew the second test after finding themselves 219 runs behind on their first innings. They batted throughout the final ten hours of the game to record 469 for 7, thereby reducing the effect of centuries by Gomes and Lloyd. Armanath, expecially, batted well for them in making 117. My pal 'Macco' Marshall at last showed signs of having developed into the effective fast bowler we knew he would someday become by taking 5 for 37 in the Indian first innings. On the other hand, I had 0 for 17 in the first innings and 1 for 81 in the long second. Was it a case between two friends of one's star rising while another's was falling? I had seen such things happen so often in the past that I began to worry. Was I over the hill? Would my right shoulder finally give out? To add to my physical troubles, I had begun to feel less confident and was not producing. I knew the warning signs. If I did nothing about it, this would be the beginning of the end of my test career.

The third test offered no consolation. The Guyanese weather is always unpredictable and during this game it was as fickle as ever. Two days and a session were lost to rain, though one of the abandoned days was blessed with the most brilliant sunshine. The problem was that the rain fell before playing time and left the ground saturated. The match was predictably drawn. Richards scored a hundred, Lloyd, playing at home for the first time since 1977, got 81 captain's runs. On the easy-paced wicket, Gavaskar got an characteristic century and Malcolm Marshall's pace was deadly. I got 1 for 57, a lucky catch by Richards at slip after the ball bounced from keeper Dujon's gloves. I felt that if my place in the side was to be secured again, I would have to do much better in the fourth test, which fortunately was to be played on my home ground, Kensington.

We won the fourth test, but I had little to do with it. Roberts bowled extremely well in taking eight wickets in the match. Haynes made 92, Richards 80, Lloyd 50 and little Gus Logie 130 in our 486 response to the Indian first innings total of 209. The Kensington wicket was as fast as ever, and the Indians, with the sole exception of Armanath, were incapable off dealing with Roberts and Marshall. They lost the game halfway through the final day although all but one half hour of the first day's play was lost to rain. In their second innings, they could manage only to even the scores and thus avoid an innings defeat. I had the fairly respectable figures of 2 for 41 in the first innings and 1 for 48 in the second; but bowling had become a chore. My heart was there but the body weak and there was nothing I could do to motivate myself to reach the levels of performance that I knew the rest of the side demanded of me. Therefore I was only slightly surprised when I was dropped for the fifth and final test.

I wasn't particularly surprised, but I was hurt. In less than a year, a career that appeared solid now seemed at best very insecure. Friends and strangers in Barbados told me that I was through, washed up. I decided that I would play no serious cricket in the summer. Instead I would relax for a while, exercise, try to get my shoulder right, and perhaps, just perhaps, I would be selected for the next tour the West Indies test team would make – in India towards the end of the year.

12

The full realization that I had been dropped from the West Indies team took some time to strike home. I was not prepared to take it lying down. There were things that had to be done and only I could do them. In spite of the pain-killing treatment I was receiving for my right shoulder, it still gave me trouble. More recently, my knees had started to act up. Still, the team was on a match-winning streak and I didn't think that I would be asked to stand down. I considered the selection instead of young Winston Davis, who had taken thirty-three wickets in the Shell Shield games, a signal that the selectors were looking for someone who would permanently replace me. During chats with the fellows from Enterprise I found myself switching the boasts expected of me in response to their taunts from what I intended to do *when* I was back in the side, to what was going to happen *if* I played again.

I started to think seriously about what I would do if I didn't play test cricket again, and there appeared to be few options. I still had contracts with Somerset and South Australia; but it didn't seem to make much sense to continue to think of playing professionally if I didn't intend to regain my place in the test side. If only my shoulder didn't hurt so much when I bowled and if only I didn't tire so quickly.

One morning I was sitting on the living room floor listening to Herbie Hancock on tape, when I made a decision. I didn't think that I was washed up; I felt that all I needed was to rest and recover full fitness. Convinced that the best time to begin anything worthwhile was the moment at hand, I immediately took off the earphones and went to the beach and began a programme of swimming and running exercises. I was not prepared to accept that my ability had deteriorated.

I set myself the goal of regaining my place for the Indian tour at the end of 1983. I went to a physiotherapist in Barbados, I weight-trained in my garage, I swam miles along the coast at Southpoint, I ran in the wet sand in the early hours of the morning, I ate Gran's cooking in huge quantities; but most of all, I exercised. I trained every moment I could. But the team to India was announced, and I was not included. I was told that I would be brought back for the series of one-day internationals that the West Indies would play in Australia immediately after the Indian tour if I had regained full fitness.

Was my exclusion from the full tour some kind of trial? Was I to be played in the one-day games before the selectors could make a decision on my form for any future test series? What level of performance would satisfy them? These questions were among those continually flying through my mind as I ran along the wet sand at Enterprise in the early hours of the morning. What would happen if I was not fully fit and they called me to Australia? Should I accept? If I didn't go, would that be the end of my test career?

Eventually, I was called to join the West Indies team for the first game in the Benson and Hedges World Series Cup to be played at Melbourne on 8 January 1984. I was overjoyed but at the same time a little worried that I might not be able to recover playing form quickly enough, since I lacked match practice.

I flew to Australia and was immediately included in the team for the first limited over game which we won by 27 runs. Batting first, we made 221 for 7 and then bowled out Australia for 194. I gave my right shoulder a good work-out and ended up with Kepler Wessels' wicket for 28 runs off 8 overs. Border, showing that he was a continuing force to be reckoned with, scored 84 not out; and, had Yallop not twisted his knee, the game could have gone the other way.

In the second game, I again got a single wicket; but this time for 21 runs off 10 overs. Nevertheless, we lost by 97 runs after our batting completely collapsed for 111 while chasing the Pakistani total of 208. For some unexplained reason, our side has consistently found it difficult to make winning scores in low-scoring matches against Indian and Pakistani teams in limited overs games. Some of our players refuse to accept that the Indians or Pakistanis can bowl us out before reaching their score, or prevent us from stopping them reaching whatever number of runs we happen to make. It is a weakness that has lost us a couple of games that we should have won, including a World Cup final.

My worst fears were realized during the second game. My knees did not hold up for the ten overs. I bowled the last two with a jarring pain in my left knee every time I followed through. After that, I missed six World Cup matches while I brooded and took pain-killers. Just when the writing appeared to be on the wall, I was selected for the last game, before the finals against Pakistan. I had something to prove to myself. The knee felt better, and the wicket at Perth was helpful. I got 2 for 12 off 9 overs, and we restricted the Pakistanis to 182 for 7 off their 50 overs. Thanks to an anchor knock of 78 not out by Desmond Haynes and scintillating 40 by Viv Richards, we won by seven wickets.

I missed the following game against Australia which we lost. However, we still led the qualifying table by a clear five points over the Australians and I was happy to be chosen for the finals against them.

The first final was a day/night game played at Sydney on 8 February. The Australians were due to leave the following week to start a five-test series against us in the West Indies and they were involved in widely publicized negotiations with their Board that could not have helped their play. For my part, I knew that my performances in the finals would be closely watched in view of the upcoming series. I hoped that my knees would hold up, and before play started in that first final I was determined to do my utmost to ensure selection.

Play began late, reducing the match to forty-six overs a side. We found the overcast conditions much to our liking, and we got the ball to move around much more than we had done previously. In spite of a solid innings of 50 from Smith, the Australians were bowled out for 160. I got 2 for 19 off 9 overs. We had the match won. Australian morale was so low that we could not imagine them bowling us out in under 160 runs. Our new find, Richie Richardson, made 80 entertaining runs. Larry Gomes produced his usual determined knock to score 46 not out. We made the 161 required to win for the loss of only Desmond Haynes' wicket.

Three days later, we went into the second final confident that we could beat the Australians and retain the Cup. Batting first, Richardson and Richards, scoring 43 and 59 respectively, helped us to 222 for 5 from our 50 overs. We had made more than enough runs to win, especially since Smith had dislocated a shoulder while fielding and Graham Richie had injured a knee while exercising before the start of the game. Jones, sent in to open, was caught behind off Holding with the score at 23, and we were ecstatic. But then Wessels and Hughes scored 109 runs before another wicket fell, and we began to see our chances of winning the game slipping away.

Crickus then confounded the Australian batting. Hughes was lbw to Marshall who then caught Wessels off Holding, and Australia were 161 for 3. The match seemed evenly balanced, but at 169 Border was caught behind off the faintest of touches and Richie fell the same way at 176. When I clean bowled Marsh at 192, I figured that we had it won. We had all their front-line batsmen back in the pavilion and they needed thirty-one runs to win. But Lawson held out, and it appeared that the Aussies would win after all.

With one run to win off the last ball of the game, Rackemann was slow to start for a single that went through to the wicket-keeper and was run out. The scores were tied. We all thought that we had won the match because we had never heard of such a thing as a tied game in limited overs cricket. We had made 222 for 5, they had made 222 for 9. We had a much better record in the preliminary games. The celebrations began.

Our glee was premature. Three hours later we were informed that the official position was that the game was tied and we would have to play another. Angrily, we decided not to do so. We felt that we were being taken for a ride. With the memory of the last New Zealand tour fresh in our minds, we thought that we were being set.

The deciding game was scheduled to be played on the following day and, aware that most of the players had agreed not to play, I did not even stay in the team's hotel that night. For me, the tour was over. Imagine my surprise when I got back to the hotel the next morning to discover that the West Indies team, including those who had been loudest in their opposition to play, had gone to the grounds. I hurriedly scraped together my gear and rushed off to see what new developments had taken place in my absence. When I got to the dressing room I was told that the Australians had decided to offer additional prize money for the game. At the team meeting, manager Wes Hall was able to convince most of us that we should not only play the match but win it convincingly if we were to be accepted as limited overs champions. In spite of this, Lloyd and Richards did not play and it was left to Holding to lead a team of angry West Indians on to the field.

I didn't particularly feel like playing. I was put off not only by having to play the game at all, but also because I felt let down by those who had decided to go ahead with the game after strong opposition the night before. I decided to blow off steam in the only legitimate way I knew. I bowled my overs and forgot friendships with some of the Australian batsmen. I forgot everything else for ten overs, during which I took five Australian wickets for thirty-one runs, and caught Jones at gully off Holding. Australia made 212 for 8; but it was not going to be easy to beat them with only four specialist batsmen.

We were given an early scare and Marshall and I exchanged glances and whispers of 'I told you so' when, with the score at 3, Haynes and Gomes fell to successive balls from Lawson, bowling as though he felt that Australia would win. Fortunately for us, Richardson and Logie had different ideas about the affair. They added 49 before Richie was lbw to Hogg for 27. Logie produced a marvellous innings of 88 with exciting shots all over the ground. By the time that he was fourth out at 176 our bowlers were resolved to score the required runs if they had to. Dujon, with a stylish knock of 82 not out, made our resolve unnecessary. We accomplished an overwhelming win by making the 213 required runs for the loss of 4 wickets with 27 balls to spare.

Bowling in anger earned me the Man of the Finals Award. More important to me, I was certain that my performance had brought me back into the side on a permanent basis. It was a very different 'Bird' that flew back to Barbados than the one who had left.

Back home, I continued to train hard and maintain my level of fitness because I knew what it meant to a fast bowler's career to be dropped from the home side playing in the West Indies.

I was not ready to leave the test scene yet. I prayed to the Old Man upstairs that my knees and shoulder would stand up to the pressure.

By the time the Australians got to the West Indies early in 1984, our side had already proven itself to be a tightly-knit unit of professionals capable of playing cricket at a very high standard. Most of us had been playing together for more than five years. Whereas in the pre-Packer days this would have meant little or nothing in terms of test cricket experience, the increase in the number of tours after 1978 allowed us to play together almost continually. We knew each other's strengths and weaknesses. We had come to recognize personality flaws, and live with them. We could have heated arguments at team meetings and then go on the field and play without concern for what had taken place earlier. We offered each other advice on how to get various batsmen out; and many were the times then a bowler at one end would make up for errors made at the other. Furthermore, the selection policy of maintaining the same nucleus of players – even when some of the key ones were temporarily out of form – and introducing new elements cautiously, strengthened the side. Malcolm Marshall, my room-mate, had been introduced in this way, and with each game he consolidated his place in the team and became an increasingly effective, extremely hostile, fast bowler.

If by 1984 we had developed into a solid team, playing as one, a certain deterioration had set in among the Australians. Before the tour, Greg Chappell, Lillee and Marsh had retired from international cricket. Graham Yallop, who had scored heavily against Pakistan in Australia's previous test series, missed the tour through injury. More injuries were to further weaken the Australian side during the series. Wessels was forced to return to Australia after the second test, and his replacement, Wood, played in the third test only and then had a finger fractured. Steve Smith also suffered a fractured finger in the fifth test and batted only one innings. Their bowling also was not immune. Rackemann played in only one test, and Rodney Hogg missed the fourth.

Initially, it seemed that injuries to fast bowlers would affect us more than it would them. Holding and Marshall were both hurt and had to stand down for the first test. When Australia batted first our bowlers knew that we would have to put in an extra effort to make up for their absence. I pulled out the stops on the slow Guyanese wicket and got three quick wickets before rain stopped play just after lunch with Australia on 55 for 3. The next day, they tumbled to 182 for 9, only reaching that score through a stubborn 78 from Richie, before Hogg and Hogan put their heads down in a record last wicket partnership of 97. In the Aussie total of 279, I took 6 wickets for 75 runs off 27 overs. I felt fit and satisfied.

If our batsmen thought that we could easily pass the Australian score, they soon had another think coming. Lawson, one of the most competitive and aggressive bowlers (if not the best behaved) had Greenidge and Richardson early on the third day. This was during a fiery spell in which he expressed the angry frustration that the previous afternoon had made him snatch his hat from an umpire who had turned down one of his frequent appeals. In spite of a laboured 60 from Dessie Haynes, we never really recovered and were finally all out for 230, 49 behind the Australians.

Wayne Daniel and I then had them with their backs against the wall at 60 for 5 in their second innings before the left-handers, Border and Phillips, brought our progress to a standstill with a partnership of 125 which only ended when Border was run out. Rain again interrupted play on the fourth day, and when on the last day we had Phillips early, Australia were 209 for 7. It still looked as though we could pull it off; but Lawson and Hogan batted well enough to afford their captain, Hughes, the pleasure of a declaration at 273 for 9.

We had to make 322 runs to win; and at one stage it looked as if we might be able to make them as Greenidge and Haynes rushed to individual hundreds, but we were left stranded at 250 without loss (Greenidge on 120 and Haynes on 103) and the match was drawn. No one knew what would have happened had so much time not been lost to the rain; but the Australians had been given fair warning that we were not going to be easy to beat and that they were going to have to spend a lot of time in the Caribbean heat chasing balls. I had given them my own little warning too with match figures of 9 for 142.

The wicket at Trinidad was not the spinners' paradise usually expected there. Viv Richards, leading the side in place of an injured Lloyd, sent the Australians in to bat after winning the toss. When our Nemesis, rain, stopped play just after lunch on the first day, Australia had scored 55 and I had carried away all four of the wickets to fall.

The next morning, our team had some measure of success by claiming the early wicket of David Hookes. Border and Jones stone-walled with an even hundred partnership; but we afforded ourselves the pleasure of preventing Border from reaching his century. I proved that I was still capable of restraining the best of them. I bowled two successive maiden overs at him when he was on 98, and he was stranded on that score when Alderman was removed and they were all out for 255. I had followed up my 6 for 75 in the first innings of the first test with 6 for 60. I had fully recovered my confidence.

When we batted, the wicket that had appeared so hostile during the Australian innings now seemed tame and easy. The early moisture had gone out of it, and Dujon, Logie and Richards took full advantage of the situation. Logie, replacing Lloyd, suffered a late attack of nerves and missed a deserved hundred when he was lbw at 97. Dujon experienced no such anxiety. He made 130 thrilling runs, including fifteen fours and two sixes which were hooks off successive balls from Hogg. Richards declared with about an hour left on the fourth day when we were 468 for 8. Wessels was trapped lbw after Phillips had been run out and they finished on 55 for 3. We looked forward to the last day when we would wrap it up.

When the eighth Australian wicket fell before tea on the last day and they had scored only 196 runs, still seventeen runs behind, I thought that we would win the game I was watching from the pavilion because I had had to leave the field with a stomach upset. But Border clung on for dear life, hitting the last ball of the match for four to bring up his century and draw the game.

With the hope of recuperating and being fit for the next test I stood down for the Barbados–Australia match. Only two of the six Barbadian players who had represented the West Indies in the second test played in the island game. The Australians played only three specialist bowlers, obviously intent on giving their batsmen much needed practice. The game was, as expected, drawn before one of the smallest crowds ever to watch a touring team at Kensington. The wicket turned out to be a wonderful batting strip. Eight Australian batsmen made more than fifty runs in the game, with Richie reaching 99 in the first innings and Hookes getting a century in the second.

In spite of the easy play of the wicket during the Barbados game, Lloyd, back to lead the side after missing the previous test, sent the Australians in to bat after winning the toss at the start of the third test. He was forced to introduce Harper's off-spin before lunch on the first day. After Smith fell at 11, having made ten of them, Wood and Richie played carefully to add 103 runs. By the close, the Aussies had reached 227 for 5. The next day, we got them out for 429, a total that would have been far smaller had we held our catches. I finished with 3 for 110 off 33 overs.

As if continuing where they had left off in the second innings of the second test, Greenidge and Haynes gave us a wonderful start of 132 before Greenidge was run out for 64. Haynes and Richardson then batted steadily to add a further 145 runs. We were still 128 runs behind when we went into the rest day at 289 for 3.

When we resumed our innings, Richardson, playing in place of Logie who had come down with the 'flu the day before the match, batted sensibly and, anxious to retain his place in the side, scored 131 not out. He is an excellent pressure batsman, also gifted with the ability to make exciting attacking strokes. He can be depended upon in the big match, unlike many young players who flatter at secondary level only to deceive when the dice are cast in a test match. Richardson is a batsman with guts and determination who seeks to succeed.

After Dujon was quickly out, Lloyd changed the slow tempo of the game by playing a swashbuckling innings of 76 during which fortune favoured the brave. Rushing to make as many runs as we could, we more or less collapsed (if that is the appropriate word under the circumstances) for 509 – ahead by 80 runs on the first innings.

By the end of the fourth day, Australia had lost 4 wickets for 68 runs. Wood was out early by the lbw route; but the terror of the Australian second innings was Marshall. On a wicket that was still favouring batsmen, he bowled as fast as I can remember. Holding provided solid support. On the final morning, the two of them cleaned up the Australian batting, taking between them 6 for 29 in just over an hour, leaving Greenidge and Haynes with the formality of scoring 18 runs to win.

Since test cricket began at the Recreation Ground in Antigua, the matches have been little more than exhibitions of Antiguan prowess before hometown crowds. The fourth Australia–West Indies Test in 1984 was no exception. The highlight of the game was a record third wicket stand of 308 runs between Richards and Richardson, the latter surviving a straightforward chance behind when he had scored 38.

The Australians, for their part, brought problems to the match that seriously hampered their performance. They had to play the game immediately after their defeat in Barbados, and could not have been fully recovered. Wood and Hogg were both injured and could not play. Australia were trying a third opening pair: Phillips and Richie. The latter was not used to opening and the former had not scored many runs in that position. They were both quickly out after Hughes won the toss and decided to bat. Border propped up the innings with a solid 98; but Australia could only muster 262 runs before the Antiguans more or less won the game with their formidable partnership that allowed us to make 498 runs. Richards hit no fewer than 30 fours in his innings of 178 during which he was dubbed 'the master blaster'.

On the fourth day I tried to glean some the praise before all went to Marshall, who got his one hundredth and one hundredth and first test wickets. Bowling as staight and as fast as one would expect, I got 5 for 63. The Australians were bowled out for 200 with extras top-scoring with 36. We had beaten them by an innings and 36 runs, secured the series and retained the Frank Worrell Trophy. The 'Bird' was flying higher than ever. The Aussies found this out in the two one-day internationals following the tests.

Sabina Park in Jamaica was all dressed up for the fifth and final test. The occasion marked the West Indies one hundredth home test. Coincidentally, it also marked the one hundredth test in which our skipper, Clive Lloyd, would be playing; the most by any West Indian cricketer. The Australians experienced what must have been a recurring nightmare: sent in to bat, four wickets fell for 73 runs by the lunch interval. Once again only Border put up any substantial resistance, this time partnered by Hookes; but their efforts were unable to stop us from running through the side, and we were batting before close on the first day having bowled out Australia for 199. Roger Harper's 2 for 26 off 20 overs plus a catch reflect the influence he had on the proceedings. I had taken 3 for 42 and Marshall 3 for 37.

The Australians might have been able to change the eventual outcome of the game if they had taken their chances when we batted. They dropped no fewer than six relatively easy chances, a couple of which enabled Greenidge and Haynes to build a foundation for our innings of an opening partnership of a hundred. They put on 162 runs before a wicket fell: Haynes's for 60. Greenidge made 127. Only steady bowling by Maguire and Hogan, and Lawson's competitive spirit, prevented us from scoring well above the 305 runs we eventually made.

Set 106 runs to avoid an innings defeat, the Australians, again with the exception of Border, seemed out of their depth. Phillips was out at the beginning and Maguire at the end; but in between, Malcolm Marshall demolished the Australian innings. He took 5 for 51 from 23 overs of pure fiery venom. Australia duly reached 160.

We were left with 51 runs to win. Greenidge and Haynes dutifully knocked them off and secured us a victory by ten wickets. We had won three out of the five tests and three of the four one-day games. Kim Hughes called us the strongest, most professional and most disciplined team he had played against, and right there, at the top of the West Indies bowling averages, was yours truly with a record thirty-one wickets for the tests at an average of about seventeen runs each.

I was probably the happiest man on the team. Dropped from the side the previous season, called washed-up even by friends I hoped hadn't meant it, plagued by recurring injuries to knees and shoulder, I still bowled 208 overs in the tests. Only Marshall, with 158, came close to that feat of endurance. Overall, the team had worked splendidly. Incredibly, we had gone through

the series without losing a single second innings wicket. I think
that only the weather prevented us from winning the first two
tests. We were bowled out for fewer than 300 runs only once.
We passed 500 once and 450 twice; and five of our batsmen
scored centuries. It was a pretty formidable combination that
England would be facing when we got there in the summer.

13

Like a well-oiled engine the West Indian team purred into England in the summer of 1984. By then, the players were used to working together and, most important, winning together. Of the sixteen, only two, Small, the young Barbadian fast bowler, and Payne, the reserve wicket-keeper, had not previously played in a test. We ended up using thirteen players in the tests because Holding was injured for the second, Marshall missed the fourth, and Milton Small had to return to Barbados through injury.

The English players, on the other hand, could hardly be considered a formidable team. They lacked cohesion and had little experience of playing together. Their selectors, unable to choose some leading players because of a three-year ban imposed for playing in South Africa, picked twenty-one players for the five tests. Their side for the first clearly reflected the nature of the problem they would face for the duration of the series. Miller, Pringle and Downton were former test players who had been left out of England's previous winter tour. They may not have been selected if the ban on other players had not been in force. Andy Lloyd, the left-handed opening batsman, was to make his debut. Randall would be asked to bat at number three, although he had a poor test record at the position. With five potential weak links, two spinners, and only one genuine fast bowler in Bob Willis, England ran the risk of falling apart whenever we applied pressure, which we certainly intended to do.

Our team spirit and commitment to success were evident as soon as we started playing in earnest. Rain brought a premature end to the first game against Worcestershire; but by then Greenidge and Haynes had kicked off the tour with a 206-run opening partnership in 227 minutes. Neither Richards nor I played in the second game against our county team Somerset; but the West Indies won by an innings and 101 runs in just over two days. Malcolm Marshall sent out an early warning that should have had alarms going off in many club houses in England by bowling extremely quickly and accurately to take 7 for 44. Roger Harper took 5 for 32 with his off-spinners in the first innings and then made 73 runs.

We went on to give Glamorgan the worst whipping they had ever received from a touring team by beating them by an innings and 226 runs. I sent out my own signals in the form of my performance during the match and felt healthier than I had done for a long time. Richards and Richardson batted as if they were in Antigua, scoring 170 and 111, respectively.

In the first couple of limited overs games, we also played superbly. We beat Lancashire by 56 runs and then England, in the first Texaco Trophy Match, by 104. In that game, Richards made a glorious 189 in an innings he himself declared to be one of the best he had ever played. It wasn't until the second Trophy match that we were beaten. England won by three wickets with two overs remaining. All our batsmen failed, with the exception of Lloyd, who made a solid 52.

We made up for that set-back by beating England in the third and final one-day, by seven wickets. Richards perked up again with 84 not out off 65 balls with poor Bob Willis taking the brunt of the punishment – as always seemed to be the case when these two met. The story goes that when they were youth cricketers, Willis once got Richards out cheaply and that was the reason why Viv used to be particularly severe on Willis' bowling.

The last two games before the first test were both drawn. The affair against the Universities was a batting spree. Haynes made 100, Richardson 88 and Logie 96. The combined talent of Oxford and Cambridge could only muster 78 in their first innings, but defended well in the second. Against Northamptonshire, Marshall got 4 for 36 and Larry Gomes made 109 not out.

By the time of the first test at Edgbaston, all of our leading players had made some significant contribution to the team's performance. We were ready for England, and not at all convinced that England were ready for us. At the team meeting before the game, many members of the side pointed out that the major obstacle to our success would be over-confidence. The bowlers knew that in order to win we would have to go after Gower, Lamb and Botham; the batsmen would have to take care of Willis.

Rain had fallen on the day before the start, and the pitch was not as quick as expected. Probably because he had included two spinners in his side and could use them to major advantage only if we batted last, the England captain Gower decided to bat after winning the toss. By lunch, we had scattered the top of the batting order and had them at 73 for 4. With only five runs on the board, Fowler was caught behind; and Randall edged a yorker into his stumps. At 45 and 49 Lamb and Gower had been caught in the slips. Botham should have gone, too; but Harper, who is usually safe as houses, put down the chance. Botham celebrated his second life with a belligerent 64, including 23 off 2 overs, and 10 fours.

Andy Lloyd batted well, getting behind the ball and playing with the full face of the bat, before he ducked into a buzzer from Marshall and was struck a terrible blow on the side of his head. He retired hurt and took no further part in the series. I got Miller to edge to Dujon, and Holding did the same to Pringle. Cook had no idea what was happening when he edged Marshall to Lloyd in the slips; and Downton, after playing one of those gritty innings (of 33) that wicket-keepers always seem capable of, was last out lbw. England had fallen for 191. The bowlers had done their job well.

Part of our strategy was for our batsmen to collar Bob Willis; but for the hour and a half that remained on the first day it looked as though he had brought the noose. In a spell of hostile and accurate fast bowling, he got Haynes lbw after the batsman had been caught off a no-ball and then beat Greenidge all ends up for pace to get him out lbw also. We were 53 for 2 at close and a bit unnerved.

The next morning, Viv played the second ball off his pads for four and then drove the fourth straight back past Pringle and we knew that, upset stomach or not, he was going to take it to the Englishmen. At the other end Gomes, playing a characteristic innings of little dabs and flicks, offered perfect support. Gomes is a tiresome batsman to bowl at. He seldom appears to be making runs because he rarely strikes the ball ferociously.

Instead, he approaches his highest scores in crab-like fashion, cautiously and rather sideways. He walks to the wicket and appears to be doing nothing for a while until you look up at the scoreboard and he's forty-something. The next moment, he's raising his bat, acknowledging applause for a century that he has reached with more stealth than a pick-pocket.

With Richards, Gomes added 206 runs before the former was caught at mid-off after 117 blistering runs. Gomes proceeded to steal his century in the last over before tea and we were 293 for 3 and looking unstoppable. After tea, Dujon was caught off bat and pad; but any joy the English team got from this success must soon have evaporated as Lloyd and Gomes added 124 runs at better than even time. Lloyd's 71 was a merciless onslaught on the bowlers. At times he can be a ruthless batsman. He struck the second new ball with all the confidence and power he possessed before mistiming a drive and being taken at first slip. Gomes was out in the same fashion for 143 well-timed, carefully put together runs. We were 418 for 6 and comfortable. Not so the Englishmen.

The following morning they faced a Caribbean hurricane in the form of a partnership of 150 between Holding (69) and Baptiste. When Holding got out, I tried to hold an end to enable Baptiste to make his first test hundred, but failed, snicking a catch to slip; and he was left not out on 87. We had made 606 runs. The second part of the play had been acted out with the batsmen taking over the starring roles. It was up to us to recapture centre stage.

England, without one of their openers and facing arrears on their first innings of 415 runs, appeared despondent. It was not my job to build up their spirits. By tea, Fowler was lbw and Randall backing away was caught at first slip. My success continued after tea when Gower cut at one wide of the off stump and edged to Dujon. England were 37 for 3 and, to all intents and purposes, on the mat.

Marshall was bowling extremely quickly at the other end. His size belies the amount of pace he is capable of generating. He hustles in to the wicket and lets fly at tremendous speed. His bouncers are lethal, partly I think, because they are unexpected. On the day he was unlucky not to have captured at least five wickets. He unnerved every batsman that faced him, and I don't think that Lamb ever saw the ball that got him out, caught in the slips.

Marshall likes a challenge. Botham is aggressive. When Botham hooked two Marshall bouncers for fours, we knew that he was playing with fire. Marshall produced two short-pitched deliveries that flew off the wicket at a frightening pace, rose threateningly towards Botham's head before the batsman was able to get out of the way, and ripped through to Dujon. Umpire Bird, for the second time in the game (the first being when Marshall tried to shake up Willis in the first innings) warned him for bowling short. When he learned why Bird was cautioning Marshall, Roger Harper, no dwarf, asked me, 'At his height how else can he bowl?' I'm sure that few Englishmen, least of all Botham, would have found that funny.

At the close on the third day, England had survived for 112 for 4. Early on the fourth, Botham was forced back and trapped lbw, thereby shattering any skimpy hope England might have entertained of pulling off a miracle. When Willis was caught behind just after lunch, England, with 235 second innings' runs, had been beaten by an innings and 180. I had gained match figures of 9 for 108. Although it had been a bit like participating in a commando raid on an undefended village, I was totally satisfied with the outcome.

The statistics reflected the difference between the two teams. Only Marshall and I had centuries scored off us in both innings together while, in our one innings, four of the English bowlers had been struck for over a hundred runs and the fifth, Miller, had been hit for 83. Only two fifties were scored by Englishmen; we had five. Our cricketing machine had ground England into the dust.

Ten days after the victory at Birmingham we were in London for the second test at Lord's. To play at the headquarters of cricket is always a thrill. I get the feeling there of being a link in a chain that stretches through time and connects me with all those who have ever played test cricket. Of all the English grounds, Lord's is most like home, especially when the sun shines and the West Indians come out in droves to support us. To beat England at Headingley, for example, is satisfying; but to beat the home side at Lord's is an experience to cherish.

Given how confident we were before the match, and our complete domination of the first test, it was something of a shock to go through almost the whole second test without ever really being decisively on top. Lloyd sent England in to bat and immediately Crickus made it clear which side he intended to support. Small (playing his first test in place of an injured Holding) Marshall and I plugged away at the left-handed openers Fowler and Broad. The first day was shortened by bad light and rain; but even when the light was good, Broad refused to see anything pitched outside the line of his off stump. He was caught twice in the slips, at 24 and 45, off no-balls from Marshall. Fowler, on the other hand, seemed to be able to see the ball outside his off stump. At least he played at them; the trouble was that he never connected.

They put on 101 runs, the longest opening partnership against us for quite some time, before Broad went for his leg glance once too often and Dujon pulled off a blinder of a catch to dismiss him. Gower, apparently in two minds whether to play forward or back, was lbw to Marshall; but England were still reasonably secure at 167 for 2 at the end of the rain-shortened day.

Any notions the Englishmen had of putting together a big score were quickly snuffed out the following morning when Marshall, bowling at a fierce pace from around the wicket, took both Lamb and Gatting lbw. Fowler reached his hundred before Baptiste got him to edge to Harper at second slip. Botham arrived threatening fire and brimstone before Baptiste threw cold water on his and England's hopes with a beauty that flew up from a good length; it was all Botham could do to steer the ball to Richards in the gully. He had made 30 and put on 58 with Fowler for the fifth wicket; but, as has frequently happened when Botham has played against us, he got out to a virtually unplayable delivery. He has come in for some heavy criticism from time to time. What many of his critics don't seem to understand is that we respect Botham's ability and try harder when he's at the crease.

In cricket, as in many other pursuits, you often have to make your own luck. Crickus does his dirty work; but sometimes you'll be surprised to find that he sides with you when you attempt the apparently impossible feat. At 250, Downton turned a ball to fine leg and set off from what appeared to be a comfortable double when Baptiste picked up the ball on the run and threw *to the bowler's end*, scoring a direct hit to run out Miller who, totally aghast, was stranded well out of his crease.

We couldn't dislodge Downton; but I got Pringle lbw and Marshall tore past the two last wickets to bowl England out for 286. When we walked off the field, Marshall and I congratulated each other on the job we had done. The night before, both of us had said that England would get somewhere between 300 and 350 runs. There had been a time when the West Indies were always expected to crumble under pressure. We were aware that we were now passing that reputation on to other sides.

Ian Botham has the natural ability to change the complexion of a game swiftly and decisively, if given the chance. If he failed with the bat, he could usually be expected to try harder with the ball. On the second day of the Lord's test, in half an hour of bustling, busy, energetic and effective fast-medium bowling, he carried away Greenidge, Haynes and Gomes for thirty-five runs. At one point, it looked as though he might be able to spearhead an English counter-attack. But by the end of the day, Lloyd and Richards had overcome the early threat and we had reached 119 for 3, a solid foundation on which we could build a match-winning total the following day.

Willis and Botham continued on the third morning to bowl an excellent line and length, containing two of the world's most aggressive batsmen. Richards was unfortunate to be given out lbw to a ball from Botham that the umpire later agreed might have been going down the leg side. Viv had made 72 and we were 183 for 3 and still not unduly troubled. Then Dujon, falling for Botham's favourite trick of encouraging the hook shot, top edged to square leg and Lloyd, after an uncharacteristically slow seven runs only added to his overnight score, misjudged a straight one and was lbw for 39. Six wickets had fallen for 173 and Botham had taken all of them. He bagged two more, Harper's and mine, to get us out for 245, an embarrassing 41 runs behind on the first innings. We only reached such relative respectability because of a seventh wicket partnership of 40 between Baptiste and Marshall, both of whom Willis claimed, thereby denying Botham a record.

Although behind on the first innings, we had no intentions of giving up. At the team meeting we were unanimous that we could win the game outright. The bowlers felt that we stood a strong chance if we bowled England out for around 250 runs. Our batsmen felt that they could make 300 in our second innings, if given time. None of them felt that Botham could repeat his first innings achievement. It came down to a matter of containing the English batting, which meant that it was up to the remaining bowlers because Small, in his first test, had been ineffective in the first innings.

We got off to a good start. In the second over, Broad got a bouncer that he could only fend to third slip where Harper clutched the ball securely. Small surprised us all by taking Gower, caught low at first slip by Lloyd, and Fowler, lbw in the same over.

Gower is one of England's best batsmen. Technically correct, he is capable of dominating play once he has settled down. He shares, with most of the leading English players, a strange vulnerability early in an innings to a ball of good length pitching on or outside the off stump and moving away. Had Gower been 50 or 60 instead of 21, the ball that got him out would most likely have been dispatched to the cover boundary. As it was, he was gone and England at the close of the third day were 114 for 4, a mere 155 in the lead. Gatting had batted well for 29 before, for the second time in the game, misjudging the line and getting out lbw to Marshall. Lamb never looked like getting out.

On an overcast fourth morning following the rest day, Botham and Lamb attempted to win back the initiative for England. They both played fine strokes in a fifth wicket partnership eventually worth only 128 runs because Lloyd set extremely defensive fields and Baptiste bowled a containing line just short of a length. Bad light stopped play for about two hours. Only twenty-eight runs came from the next fourteen overs. Bowling at Botham, Baptiste had the remarkable figures of 10 overs for 10 runs.

Botham was finally out, more because of his frustration at the slow pace of the proceedings than the difficulty of handling that particular delivery. He had stepped back to force the ball through mid-wicket and played across the line. When he left, we tried to break open the game. Small got Downton lbw with a yorker into his boot and Harper bowled Miller. Lamb, having reached his century, surprisingly agreed to a stoppage for bad light with an hour's play left.

On the final morning of the game, Lamb managed to add only one run to his overnight score before he went for a drive off Marshall and edged to Dujon behind the stumps. It was an irony that emphasized the absurdity of the previous evening's decision. After Pringle was lbw, Gower declared with England 300 for 9, giving us 342 runs to win in five and a half hours. When we discussed strategy before our second innings began, it was decided to go for victory. If England should achieve a significant breakthrough by taking a couple of key wickets quickly, we would shut up shop and settle for the draw. When Lloyd asked Greenidge if he thought we could make the runs, the opener answered, 'How you mean if we can make them?'

Lloyd said, 'Then don't get out.'

Greenidge replied that if we continued to pick up singles and the odd boundary then we should be all right.

The man was serious. In the first hour of our second innings, he put on 57 runs with Haynes before the latter was run out when he slipped after being sent back. He had made 17. When Haynes reached the pavilion and Lloyd asked him if it was still worth going after the runs, he agreed that it was. He added that Greenidge was in good shape. At lunch, we had scored 82 from 20 overs. Greenidge had struck 10 fours in 54.

Greenidge batted almost perfectly in the period between lunch and tea. He relentlessly pursued the English bowlers, especially our Nemesis of the first innings, Botham. With Gomes imperturbable at the other end, he put on 132 runs, and passed his century with the score at 149. At tea, he had reached 125, while Gomes, the wizard of the wily innings, had sneaked to 52. We were 214 for 1 and a mere 128 runs away from our goal. During the break, we decided to turn on the heat immediately in order to prevent a mad rush at the end of the day when the light would certainly be worse.

Greenidge and Gomes responded to Lloyd's instructions in the most forthright fashion. In the first hour after tea 85 runs were added, taking us to 299 without further loss. At the start of the mandatory twenty overs, with Greenidge 186 and Gomes 75, we needed only forty-three runs to win; but the batsmen apparently wanted to bring it home as quickly as possible. The 43 came in 8.1 overs with Lord's witnessing the kind of fireworks display seldom seen there. The brightest skyrocket was when Greenridge passed his first double-century in a test with a hooked six off Foster. In all, our batsmen had hit 2 sixes and 44 fours from 66.1 overs, scoring at a rate of just over 5 runs per over. We had won. We had won. The West Indian spectators went wild with delight.

If the second test had been Greenidge's; the third belonged to Malcolm Marshall. Rarely has a test cricketer displayed the guts, determination, unselfishness and raw ability that Marshall did at Headingley. He had bowled only six overs – for six runs – when he was struck on the thumb fielding at gully and he sustained a double fracture. His left hand was put in plaster and the team doctor advised him not to take further part in the game.

England batted first for the third consecutive time and for the third consecutive time found themselves in early trouble. They were 68 for 3 at lunch. Fowler and Gower were out lbw, neither of them offering shots to inswingers, and Harper had taken a brilliant low slip catch to get rid of the newcomer, Terry, off Holding. Half an hour after the interval, Broad was caught in the slips off Harper, and England had slumped to 87 for 4. Lamb and Botham tried to muscle their way out of the sorry situation and almost succeeded. They added 85 runs at a furious pace before Botham was caught behind off the glove when he appeared to be set for a big score.

Downton provided the support that Lamb needed after Botham had gone. Together they added 64, with Lamb scoring by far the majority of the runs before Downton edged to slip and bad light stopped play forty-five minutes before the close. By then, Lamb had passed his second consecutive century, providing ample evidence that our bowling could be scored against if the batsman applied himself.

The next morning, Lamb lacked the concentration of the previous day and was bowled attempting a lazy cut to Harper's second ball. Holding then cleaned up the tail, taking the remaining three wickets to reach the 200 mark in tests. The last four wickets put on only thirty-three runs and England reached 270 all out.

The over-confidence that we constantly warned each other

about then seriously affected our batsmen. After making 344 for 1 in the second test, they appeared to take 270 very lightly. Greenidge got a good outswinger from Willis and was caught in the slips; but the way the majority of our other wickets fell to the fast-medium stuff that Allott bowled was nothing short of disgusting. Haynes was bowled attempting a coaching book off-drive. The perfect stroke, its only shortcoming was that it failed to connect with the ball. Richards went for a drive that got him caught at mid-on. Gomes and Lloyd brought some sanity back to the proceedings and added 70 runs before the skipper fell to a bat-pad catch at silly point. Though Dujon added 53 with Gomes, he never looked in form and was eventually out lbw playing badly across the line of a straight ball from Allott. Baptiste was caught at extra cover attempting to copy Haynes' perfect effort, and Harper was caught behind second ball. In the half hour remaining to stumps, Holding lashed out for twenty-eight runs including two successive sixes off Willis.

Throughout the disaster that our first innings had become, only Gomes showed any common sense or appreciation of the situation. He batted carefully and steadily to be 79 not out at the end of the day. The next morning, Holding continued where he had left off by hitting Willis for three more sixes in what was to be that hapless bowler's last test match. He did achieve some kind of revenge when Holding was caught off him at fine leg attempting another bold hook. At the other end, Gomes had moved on to 95 and fully deserved a century. I tried to give him the bowling so that he would get his ton; but instead I was run out attempting an impossible second run.

I was sorry that I hadn't been able to stick around long enough for Larry to get his century; but I was cheered, though surprised, when, on my way back to the pavilion, I saw Marshall coming down the steps. His left hand in plaster, his face a mask of determination; but in his rush to get to the wicket before everyone came off he had forgotten his box! Gomes showed his appreciation for Marshall's gesture by reaching his hundred, and Marshall even had the pleasure of a one-handed slice shot past third man for four before he was caught at slip off Allott, who finished with 6 for 61. We had made 302, a lead of 32, and Larry Gomes had made 104 sensible runs without getting out.

Our bowlers resented what we considered was our batsmen's

carelessness. In our post mortem we came to the conclusion that we had made Allott look good; that we had to work hard for six wickets in an innings and here we were giving an opposing bowler that bag as easily as ever. When Lloyd asked Marshall how he felt about bowling in the second innings, Marshall's reply was, 'I bowl with my right hand, not my left. And I know what I have to do.'

When we got on the field, Lloyd tossed the ball to Marshall; more, I think, to determine whether he could bowl at all in his condition than because he expected anything dramatic. After covering the white plaster on his left forearm with pink tape, Marshall proceeded to bowl as straight and controlled from around the wicket as anyone could. In his second over, he forced Broad to end a wicked delivery from his rib cage into the hands of Baptiste at short leg. At the other end, I struck Terry plumb in front and England were 13 for 2.

Gower and Fowler tried to stem the tide. They added 91 useful runs for England; but whereas Gower always looked capable, Fowler looked as though he could get out at any time. Ironically, Gower was the first to go, caught behind chasing a wide delivery from Harper. Then Fowler attempted a drive off Marshall and was brilliantly caught and bowled by the one-armed bandit. England's 106 for 4 became 107 for 5 when Marshall totally confused Lamb and had him lbw. Just before the close, I tried one going away from Botham's off stump and he obligingly touched it to Dujon. At the end of the third day they were 135 for 6.

Marshall gave England no respite on the fourth morning. Bowling off a shortened run, concentrating on movement rather than pace, he was as accurate as a marksman. Every now and then he would get the ball to fly towards the batsman's ribs, challenging him to hook or pull. They didn't or couldn't; and he took the last 4 wickets for 15 runs off 4 overs. Only Downton, last man out, attempted to stave off the inevitable. England made 159 and we were left with 128 to win.

Marshall responded to the congratulations offered him in our dressing room for his 7 for 53 and we had our usual pep-talk about chasing small totals. It worked. Greenidge and Haynes made 106 for the first wicket. In getting the runs, we lost only the openers, and had won the third consecutive test. We began to joke among ourselves about a possible clean sweep.

At Old Trafford, we batted first for the first time in the series and, by lunch, had been forced to replace thoughts of clean sweeps with ways of avoiding embarrassment. Haynes fell to Botham's 'rope a dope' of two backward square legs and a short-pitched delivery. Gomes, Richards and Lloyd, apparently forgetting what had happened at Headingley, all yielded to Allott's temptation. We were 70 for 4.

Fortunately for us, Botham repeatedly bowled short and wide on the slow wicket. Greenidge and Dujon, taking full advantage of this, helped themselves to 121 runs between lunch and tea. After the interval, both of them completed centuries. Dujon fell immediately after his hundred when he top-edged an attempted hook off Botham at 101; but Greenidge, partnered for the last five minutes before the close by the night-watchman Davis, was 128 not out at the close.

On a normal English bleak and overcast second day, Davis, making full use of the unexpected opportunity granted when he had been called into the team from Glamorgan to replace Small, batted splendidly for 77 and added nearly 200 runs with Greenidge, before being bowled by Pocock. Following his double at Lords, Greenidge made 223 and only got out towards the end of the run-feast when trying to pile them up too quickly. We made an even 500.

The third day was even more gloomy than the second had been. Play was delayed until after lunch by a persistent drizzle, and it was cold. We didn't find the conditions suitable for playing cricket and it took us some time to get into gear after play started. Broad and Fowler amassed 90 for the opening partnership while our bowlers struggled to get them out. Once we found it, however, the situation changed dramatically. From being 92 for 1 at tea, England slipped to 163 for 5 in the final session.

Davis bowled very well indeed. He made the most of Marshall's absence to show his worth. Fowler, when on 8, had ducked into a short one from him and was badly struck on the back of the helmet and knocked off his feet. Terry was struck on the forearm and forced to retire hurt. Broad just managed to shove away a snorting chest-high bouncer to be caught on the rebound at fourth slip. Lamb ducked into a whistling delivery, and Botham, hooking, was lucky not to have been caught at slip. At one end Davis kept the Englishmen in a serious predicament and at the other Baptiste had Gower caught behind and I got my hands to a fierce slash by Botham off the same bowler. I replaced Davis and benefited from Harper's brilliant catch in the slips to remove Downton. At the close of play, England were still 137 away from avoiding the follow-on.

The weather on the fourth day made up for the previous three bleak days we had endured. It was warm and sunny. Lamb was 27 and Allott 10. Soon after the second new ball was taken, Allott fell to a miscued hook off Davis; but Lamb, with defensive support from Cook and Pocock, brought England within reach of the runs they needed to avoid the follow-on. Holding bowled Cook, Pocock and Cowans were out just after lunch. Lamb was 98 and England needed 22 to make us bat again. Terry came in to do a Marshall, with his left arm in plaster and a team-mate needing a few runs to reach a hundred. When Lamb reached his hundred off the last ball of a Holding over, we were in no charitable mood. The second yorker went past Terry's bat and England were all out for 280

When England were put back in, they lost Fowler to Holding's second ball; and we applied full pressure to the downcast batsmen who followed. It was Roger Harper, though, and not the fast bowlers, who did the damage. By the close of the fourth day, he had taken four wickets, and our opponents were 120 for 5 chasing 220. On the final day, only Gower, playing a face-saving captain's innings of 57 not out, put up much resistance. we bowled them out for 156. Roger Harper got 6 for 57. This splendid achievement can only be fully appreciated when you consider that, unlike off-spinners in other sides, he doesn't usually get the chance to bowl long spells to find his length, line and rhythm. But the most exciting thing was that England were four-love down in the series.

Our batting once again gave us an early scare in the fifth test at the Oval. After Lloyd won the toss and decided to bat, we slipped to 64 for 3 at lunch and slid to 70 for 6 soon afterwards. We depended on Lloyd to steady the innings, and his 60 not out prevented us from crumbling to an even more humiliating score than the 190 we made. I was proud of the way in which the tail supported the skipper; but thoroughly mad at the specialist batsmen who had been out earlier.

We were not very happy at having to operate under the constraint of low first-innings score, and sorry that the only way I could take out my frustration was on the opponents; but it served as a kind of motivation. I think that pressure brings out the best in me. There have been times when Marshall and I have psyched ourselves up by telling each other that if the other side's bowlers could get our batsmen out for miserable scores, then we were capable of reducing theirs to an even lower total. That is another kind of motivation. Both kinds of stimuli have the same result: I think we are far more menacing when we have only a few runs behind us.

When England batted late on the first day, Broad didn't have a chance when the ball took his off stump. The second day was almost all Marshall. Fully recovered from the injury that had kept him out of the fourth test, he bowled with the now fully-developed fury that had been simmering in previous years. Pocock, who had been sent in as night-watchman, had a torrid time of it for about an hour before he pushed a Marshall bouncer to the slips. Fowler was surprisingly put down by Harper; but then Marshall produced an express that struck his forearm and forced him to retire. Holding, coming on for Marshall, kept the temperature rising. Gower received a bouncer of disconcerting speed and lift that he was only just able to glove to the keeper, as did Tavare.

Marshall then came back after his rest to dismiss Botham and Lamb in the same over. The way these two got out spoke volumes about the difficulties the Englishmen were having with Marshall's bounce and pace. Botham got a fierce flyer that nicked his gloves in front of his face, while Lamb was lbw to a scorcing shooter. England were 84 for 6, similar to our first innings' situation, but, unlike us, they had no Lloyd to bat purposefully. We cleaned them up for 162.

At our team meeting before the third day's play began, our skipper insisted on the need for the batsmen to put their heads down and give us some runs to bowl at if we were to take the opportunity of becoming the first team to achieve a clean sweep in a test series in England.

For some time on the fourth day it looked as if our batsmen

were trying all right; but not to do what we had agreed upon. At 69 for 3 Lloyd once again had to pull things together. Greenidge was out quickly. We had come to expect great things from him every time he stepped to the crease. Gomes snicked for the third successive time, and Richards continued to experience abysmal form and worse luck. Lloyd, determined to leave test cricket in England with a big score, was visibly disappointed when he got out at 36. Dujon captivated the crowd with a series of dazzling strokes in his 49 before he predictably edged to slip.

While all was flash and departure at one end, Desmond Haynes soldiered on determinedly at the other. After a few anxious moments in the nineties, he reached his hundred with two consecutive fours. We had recovered to 284 for 7, a lead of 312; quite a few less than I thought we would need to beat England.

Our lead was extended to 374 on the fourth morning, mainly because Holding and I slashed around lustily after Haynes had dragged a ball from Botham into his stumps. England would have to bat for almost two days to avoid defeat. Marshall was not going to have any of that. He had Fowler caught at second slip with the score on 15. Broad and Tavare withstood his fury for a couple of courageous hours. Then after tea, Holding, using his long run for the first time in the series, conceded five runs from three overs and dismissed Broad, Gower and Lamb in the process. Half an hour before the close of play, I began my second innings' contribution. Tavare edged to second slip when it looked as if he might want to bat 'til kingdom come. England started the last day at 151 for 5.

After about half an hour's play on the last day of the last test I made a further contribution. Botham attempted to hook one of my bouncers but succeeded in top edging to long leg instead. Barring rain and Crickus' intervention, it was then only a matter of time. I got a couple more wickets, including Ellison, the last to fall, to bring my tally to four. And this brought the curtain down on the first ever clean sweep in a test series in England.

The exhilarated, jubilant West Indian spectators rushed on to the field in tidal wave of bodies, making the players' departure a dangerous struggle through a riotous crowd of souvenir seekers. They were later justifiably accused of overdoing the celebrations. I could be tolerant of their behaviour. If I had noticed a grown man weeping when we lost, then I would expect pandemonium when we won. West Indies–England test series are live dramas to the West Indian immigrants in Britain. These Black people are often the underdogs in their chosen homeland. A West Indies–England test match represents a situation when they are treated on equal terms. They identify with the team. For them, it did not matter that our side had played vastly superior cricket to our opponents, the underdogs had just soundly thrashed the overdogs. It was time to party.

14

The English batsmen's failure to come to terms with our persistently aggressive fast bowling was the most telling feature of the 1984 clean sweep of England. It had been our series; and by that I mean that it had been a series for the most part dominated by our fast bowling. For this reason, the weather – and it was overall a surprisingly dry summer for England – and our close-to-the-wicket catching, which was often astonishing, played vital parts in our success. Throughout the series, I always felt that our bowlers could get the team out of any trouble.

Because we had played such an important role in so devastating a defeat of the English team, our fast bowlers were the focus of much criticism from the English press. Some writers came as close as self-respect would allow to saying that our raw ability provided an unfair advantage. Others, not renowned for objectivity in assessing situations involving the English team, offered unsolicited suggestions supposed to improve the quality of the game. These included lengthening the wicket, restricting the number of short-pitched deliveries in an over, and imposing penalties for failure to achieve mandatory daily over rate. It was never made clear whether these proposals were intended to improve the quality of test cricket, or merely improve England's chances of winning. When I came across some of these notions in the press, I paid them the same sort of attention that I would to the idea that the net at Wimbledon's centre court should be lowered because a particular player consistently served double faults.

The criticism most often levelled against us was that our over rate should be improved. Some ingenuous reporters even claimed that the slow rate was a form of cheating because it allowed us to rest. I doubt that anyone who had ever played competitive cricket could have thought that one up. Apart from implying that our rate was purposefully slow, which was ridiculous, these reporters ignored the fact that we often won well within the scheduled five days of a test and that we always bowled many more no-balls than our opponents.

It was clear to me that some reporters were up to their old tricks. I remembered stories told in Barbados about how Ramadhin and Valentine had mesmerized England's batting in 1950. The lbw was changed with the result that the two spin geniuses were innocuous on their return tour of 1957. The reporters obviously wanted the English team to be at the top of the cricketing world without the hard work it takes to get there. Instead of proposing ways of emasculating our attack, it would have made more sense for them to prod the MCC into grooming a fast attack of their own. For a start, they could resist the temptation to call for individuals to be sacked after temporary lapses of form.

English criticism did not bother us unduly. We put it down to the fact that they were bad losers. Even in their euphoric praise, there was usually an element of sour grapes. They compared us with historic teams, and some even called us the best ever. Underlying these compliments, of course, was the assumption that it would take a truly great team to beat England five-love. Towards the end of the 1984 English tour, I was often asked or told how good we were. Even among team members there was disagreement when we discussed this topic, which was not often. Some of us felt that we could beat the best; others felt that we had not played the best; and a few, including me, felt that we had beaten those we had played, and that was all that could be said about it.

We predicted a much tougher tour and greater tests of our true strength when we visited Australia at the end of the year. Already the news from down under was that the Australians had developed the nucleus of a side that could challenge the more exaggerated claims being made about us.

When we arrived in Australia at the end of 1984 for the West Indies first full tour since the painful five-one defeat in 1975–6, it was clear that the five-month stay would be thoroughly exhausting. The schedule included five tests, six first-class matches, the limited overs World Championships, and a few county games. Furthermore, the matches promised to be hard-fought because the Australians were unlikely to give up meekly in the face of our glowing reputations.

From the very beginning of the first test at Perth, we got a taste of what we could expect from our opponents. By tea on the first day, we found ourselves on the defensive at 104 for 5, after being sent in to bat. On the second day, we pulled ourselves out of the mess, mainly through courageous centuries from Dujon and Gomes, both of whom were painfully struck by fast bowlers during their innings. Both of them batted with guts and determination and we accumulated 416 runs. The Australians had exposed a glaring and serious weakness: they dropped no fewer than seven catches.

After they had bowled us out Australia had just over an hour to bat on the second day. Bowlers relish situations like that because it means that they can go all out in a single burst without worrying about having to run around all day afterwards. Marshall forced Dyson to edge to slip where he was caught off the last ball of the first over. One of the key differences between the two teams was then established when we benefitted from two fantastic catches. First, Lloyd took an edge off Wood's bat inches from the ground at slip; then Holding incredibly held on to a slash from Wessels high above his shoulder at gully.

The third day was a horror I think the Australian players would love to forget. I'm certain that their captain, Kim Hughes, regretted talking to the press the evening before and assuring everyone that he would refuse to play a hook shot before their score was well past 300. He came to the wicket and hooked wonderfully, but straight into Marshall's hands on the long-leg boundary. The rest of their innings was a shambles. Holding and Marshall pushed them over like dominoes, sweeping them aside for 76, the lowest Australian score in a test against the West Indies. We sent them back in and they hardly had time to recover from the shock when Wessels edged to slip just before lunch, with their score at 4.

After lunch, I couldn't find my rhythm at all. I was not trying to bowl particularly fast; but I kept overstepping the crease. The more careful I tried to be in my run-up and delivery stride, the more ragged I became and I was no-balled eleven times in five overs. By tea, Australia had staged a minor recovery to add 90 runs without losing another wicket. During the interval, we had a chat to discuss what was happening on the field. None of us felt that Australia had a chance of avoiding defeat; but we were concerned that our earlier slickness had vanished and we had fielded sloppily in the lunch–tea period.

The discussion helped. We got four more wickets before the close while they added only 60 or so runs. Marshall bowled Dyson; and Walsh, the young Jamaican fast bowler playing in his first test, who had bowled tidily without success, was finally rewarded with the wickets of Wood and Yallop. The Australians were 158 for 5 on the third evening and they faced a daunting task. We destroyed any hopes they harboured by taking 4 wickets for 3 runs in about ten minutes on the fourth morning. Removing Phillips and Rackemann; Marshall got Hughes and Hogg. Lawson and Alderman played straight and sensibly to put on 59 for the last wicket. Perhaps they salvaged some pride, but the game had been lost much earlier. When holding had Alderman caught in the slips, they were 228 all out and soundly beaten by an innings and 112 runs.

The Australians had felt that they could beat us, and badly wanted to. When it became clear that they would fail, their frustration strained relations between the two sides. Normally aggressive, the Australians became cranky as well. It was clear from early in the first test that the tour was going to be grim.

We intended to keep the pressure on during the second test because we felt that if we broke their will then, it would be difficult for them to recover before the series ended. With the weather overcast on the first morning, Lloyd sent the Australians in to bat and immediately Wessel was clean bowled. It was about the seventh time I'd taken his wicket in nine innings. He is a solid opening batsman; but with a tendency to favour off-side strokes. Using a bit of reverse psychology, we had made up our minds to concentrate, when bowling at him, on a line just outside his off stump. We hoped that this would give him false confidence, but at the same time keep him feeling a little insecure because he would always be expecting us to change the line. I think we got him out many times because he had made up his mind that we would finally bowl at his legs and the momentary lapse when he found the ball once again drifting to off made him edge to slip or miss the ball entirely.

Holding got Dyson and Wood after the two of them looked like they might provide the kind of stability the Australian innings lacked. Holding struck Dyson twice on the thigh pad and then Dyson refused to get right across to the third delivery which he edged to the keeper. In the next over Wood's third hook stroke went straight to Marshall at fine leg. Australia were 33 for 3.

Hughes at first looked relaxed, but his inability to resist the hook stroke once again proved his downfall. He again hooked to Marshall at fine leg. Phillips then tried to hit his team out of trouble, and succeeded remarkably well, making forty-four quick runs, mostly off me, taking five of his eight fours off short-pitched balls outside his off stump, three of them off consecutive balls. It took Walsh to get him to edge behind. Marshall removed Border and Boon in quick succession, and I came back to clean bowl Lawson and then wrap up their innings at 175 by having Holland caught behind, my two hundredth test wicket.

By the close of Play on the first day we had made 65 for the loss of only Haynes' wicket, and the match was beginning to look like the walk-over of the first test. But on the second day Greenidge left at 99, after a blistering display of strokes had been quelled primarily by Lawson, and Gomes followed at 129. Richards and Dujon never got going and we found ourselves only nine runs ahead with the last specialist batsmen, Richardson and Lloyd, together.

At the time, it appeared that another golden opportunity provided by the bowlers would be tossed away by the batsmen. Lloyd had other ideas. He played an innings of brute force, although he had badly injured a finger the previous afternoon when taking a slip catch. He hit the fast bowlers all over the place, and when the decision was made to bring back the spinner Holland, he lifted him on to the roof of the pavilion. He ended the day on 109 not out, and was ably supported by Richardson who, with the help of Crickus, made 138 before his luck departed and Phillips held on to a difficult catch to dismiss him.

Marshall, of course, had no intention of allowing the initiative the bowlers had provided to slip from our grasp. He cut loose for 6 fours in 35. The next morning he went on to 57 after Lloyd inexplicably went into the doldrums and added only five runs to his overnight score. Lawson restricted our total to 424 by taking the last three wickets to fall. Lawson proved himself an extremely competitive fast bowler. Among the Australians, he was the one who thought that they could beat us. He never gave up; and perhaps it was the amount of adrenalin in his play that at times made him behave like a spoiled brat.

The Australians appeared tired and distraught. I felt that our first innings lead of 249 would prove formidable. Wessels and Dyson gave them a better start than they could have expected. Wessels especially, having finally convinced himself that we were concentrating on his off stump and not merely trying to set him up, played some telling blows past point. By lunch on the third day he had reached 42, and we had decided that it was time to change the line when bowling at him. He made only nineteen more runs before both openers left in successive overs.

With Walsh, who had suffered an injury while batting, out of the firing, the rest of that day belonged to Marshall. Although Holding took the wickets of Border, Hughes and Phillips, it was a keen Marshall, with a spell of fifteen consecutive overs of controlled thunder, who brought Australia to their knees. At the start of the fifth day, Australia were still 115 runs away from an innings defeat with half their wickets gone. Boon batted well and Lawson stepped back onto his stumps twice without being given out. But they nonetheless succumbed for 271, and left us with the formality of scoring 23 runs to win. We lost two wickets in reaching that total, but Lawson's belligerence not withstanding, the game was over.

Kim Hughes, in a gesture of self-sacrifice, offered his resignation from the Australian captaincy immediately after the second test. It was a sad event when he announced his decision, made even more tragic when he broke down while reading a prepared statement. Kim was not solely to blame for the Australian defeat. He is a gifted batsman, and, in my estimation, a good captain. He simply did not have the support required to press us. Unfortunately for him, very few of the commentators fully appreciated what he had been up against, but he was not the first captain to suffer.

In test matches we always singled out the key players as

pressure points in the opponent's team. We knew that a team's performance depended upon its morale, and that this in turn depended to a large extent upon the success of its key players. We always tried to restrict the batsman–captain to low scores. If this succeeded, it invariably led to uncertainty in the ranks and the leader's own security. Our batsmen would try to take care of the rare captain, like Bob Willis, who was a bowler. This strategy often worked, primarily because we had the overall ability to put it into effect. It was a little depressing however, when it led to the total demoralization of a player with Kim Hughes' talents.

The third test commemorated the centenary of the Adelaide Oval; but the game itself was a rather mundane affair. Lawson got among the wickets although the Australians dropped more catches than a test side serious about winning should do; Greenidge scored 95 in our first innings and Gomes 120 not out in the second after getting 60 in the first. Richards was out for a duck, continuing a spell of disconcerting low scores (not always a bad thing for top players); Marshall again blasted through the Australian batting, taking ten wickets in the game, and yours truly managed 3 for 119. We won by 191 runs, and our winning streak had begun to give the impression that we were invincible.

The fourth test was drawn, mainly because the Australians had at last found an opener. Hilditch was capable of withstanding the initial fury of our pace attack and our second innings' declaration just failed to leave us enough time to bowl them out in their second innings when they needed 370 runs to win. Hilditch scored 70 and 113. Without him, the Australians would doubtless have lost the match.

But they probably would not have been in the perilous straights they encountered on the easy-paced wicket in the first place had it not been for a splendid double century by Viv Richards. Remarkably unlucky, and without a big test score in the previous English series nor in the first three tests, he regained form explosively to give the Melbourne spectators an illustration of the art of batsmanship at its best.

By the middle of the match, tempers were flying. The tension and frustration the Australians were experiencing exploded in an altercation between Lawson and Greenidge at the beginning of our second innings. Having had an lbw appeal refused, the fast bowler verbally abused the batsman when he took his wicket soon afterwards. During the interval Greenidge asked Lloyd's permission to go to the Australian dressing room – not to complain about the exchanges with Lawson as we all expected, but to tell an awed fast bowler what would happen off the field if the standard of behaviour on it did not improve. By then, though, the series had been decided and we played the remainder of the matches in a more relaxed mood.

I felt relieved that we did not have to face the myth that a clean sweep of Australia, following our achievement against England, would have generated. I thought that it would have done our needs and our confidence absolutely no good at all.

Having been brought back to earth by the failure to win a test, I was then taken to strange, unexpected heights by off-the-field events. Lying half naked on the bed in my hotel room in Melbourne listening to Grover Washington on my tape deck, I took a phone call in which I was told that I had been awarded the MBE. At first I thought that there had been some mistake, and I asked if the other members of the team had received any phone calls. I could not understand why a single player in a team sport should be individually honoured.

The voice at the other end of the line which purported to be that of some officer of the Barbados Council was so authoritative that, although I was not completely convinced of its message, I pulled on my trousers. I was asked to be discreet about the whole thing; and actually still did not believe it when the official announcement was made. It later turned out that Gordon Greenidge had also been offered the MBE. It was not until much later when I was presented with a scroll and medallion at a short, dignified ceremony at Government House in Barbados that I accepted that I had been granted a major honour for propelling a ball at high speed in the general direction of hel- meted men. To be honoured for achievements in sport while still actually a player is a considerable distinction and I must say thanks to all those players who have made me what I am today.

Who would have imagined it? Joel Garner, the 'Big Bird' from Enterprise, who could easily have led an ordinary life, was a Member of the British Empire. It did not matter to me that the sun had long ago set on that particular empire. I was proud, though not overwhelmed. To celebrate, we lost the fifth and final test in Australia by an innings. I got 2 for 101 and Gordon Greenidge scored 18 and 21. Perhaps that suggests what honours do for practising professional sportsmen!

15

On reflection there may be a number of reasons why we experienced that sobering loss to Australia in the fifth test of the 1984–5 tour. Firstly, we left out Roger Harper from the side although the Sydney wicket had shown signs that it would take spin from early in the game. Instead, we stuck to our format and played four fast bowlers on a wicket that gave us no help whatsoever and we were mauled for 471 in the Aussie first innings. Secondly, with the exception of Clive Lloyd, our batsmen fared badly against the spin of Holland and Bennett.

Towards the end of the tour which was one of our longest, we had become so tired and fed up with cricket day after day that we had to summon up mental reserves to get through to the finals of the Benson and Hedges World Series Cup in the limited overs competition. We reached the finals relatively easily, almost on automatic pilot; but once there, we met an Australian team that, having won the last test, knew that it could beat us given favourable circumstances. They started well by winning the first game of the best of three series by twenty-six runs.

It should be said that they were improving and gaining confidence, and to a certain point complacency was setting in. Our bowlers were hammered by Aussies during their innings. In our innings, only Richards and Marshall responded to the challenge; and the former had three chances in making 68 runs. The situation had deteriorated to such a hopeless point that by the time I joined Marshall and put on 63 for the ninth wicket the game had long since slipped beyond our grasp.

In the second game, the revived Australian team came close to taking the championship outright. On a friendly Melbourne wicket, their openers put on 135 runs in 30 overs. Smith made 54 and Wood 81. I am certain that Border and the Australian selectors wished that the test match innings, especially the earlier ones, could have started with such impetus. Phillips, at the end of their innings, continued the momentum with an attacking 56 off just 37 balls, striking 7 fours, three off the last three balls he faced. For the first time in one-day internationals, I had more than 60 runs knocked off my 10 overs, as did Marshall.

We faced the herculean task of making 272 runs to win and keep the championship open after failing to reach 242 in the previous game. Given that our team was not at all in the mood for losing any more cricket at that stage of the tour, it was amazing how we put up a fight. Desmond Haynes and Richie Richardson gave us a sound start of 78 in 16 overs, and when Haynes was out Gomes continued our pursuit with a fine 47. Then O'Donnell got Richardson and Gomes, and Lawson dismissed Richards and Lloyd, and we were 176 for 5, needing another 96 runs at just over seven runs an over. It certainly didn't look good.

Then Gus Logie produced the sort of limited overs innings of which we knew the little man with the tremendous energy was capable. He struck the ball to all parts of the ground with a power and authority that belied his diminutive stature. With Dujon, all dynamic grace, he ran as if playing 'firms' in the Caribbean. Logie survived chances at 28 and 32; but so attractively aggressive was his batting that he deserved to have luck on his side as he proceeded to score 60 before hitting his wicket off the last ball of the forty-ninth over.

We needed seven runs off the last over to clinch victory. Dujon relieved the building tension by forcing Hogg through the covers for two blisetering boundaries off successive deliveries to bring us home. I later learned that when Dujon made the winning runs, people listening to the ball-by-ball broadcast in the West Indies in the wee hours of the morning came out into the streets to party. The excitement in our camp was overwhelming.

Given the unexpected chance to retain the World Cup, we played very much better in the last game although the result was a bit anti-climactic after the previous two close games. Back at Sydney, where Australia had won the last test and the first limited overs game, we bowled them out for 178, and coasted to 179 for 3 with Haynes and Richards belligerently making the same score of 76. A highly successful, though fatiguing, series was over.

In spite of some rather tense moments on the field, we had enjoyed the Australian tour. I made new friends and strengthened old friendships. I spent a lot of time with Rudi Webster and his family and through discussions with them and some promotional work in which I was engaged at the time my developing interest in a social work career grew. Up until then my dream had been to become a policeman; but that line of work now seemed impossible, primarily because I was not getting any younger. Towards the end of the Australian tour I began again to consider what I would do when the right arm stopped coming over smoothly. More and more it seemed as if some form of social work in Barbados would suit me; and therefore took whatever opportunities came my way in Australia to learn about the career and started making plans towards gaining qualifications. I probably still had a couple more tours in me; but I wasn't about to fool anybody, least of all myself, my career as a test cricketer was coming to an end.

After the Australian tour, though, there remained a couple of old scores to settle; the immediate one being with a certain New Zealand team that was to tour the West Indies in March. We were all looking forward to playing against the only side to take a series from us in recent years. All of us, that is, except Clive Lloyd who had retired from test cricket at the end of the Australian tour. We knew that we would miss the skipper both as leader and as player. Lloyd was a true international professional: a batsman on whom we could depend and an excellent close fielder. Those who knew him in his youth also remembered him as one of the very best cover fielders the game has seen. As a tactician and captain he was second to none. His willingness to offer advice and help the younger members of the side was unsurpassed. He cared about the players on the West Indies team. He was almost single-handedly responsible for shaping us into the match-winning force we had become.

When I got back to Barbados to rest and recuperate after the Australian grind, I was unhappy to find Gran weak and looking a lot older. I could not remember her being too frail to look after the animals or engage me in long conversations. She reassured me that all would be well; but I was concerned because I could see that the light in her eyes had dimmed a little. I was afraid that I might lose her; but she was still as tough as nails and she whispered to me not to worry about her, that she would be all right.

I looked after Gran as best I could for the days that I had left before the tests against the New Zealanders started. I had a great deal of help from the nurses who were our next-door neighbours, and was able to avoid depression and maintain my physical fitness.

Viv Richards had been chosen to lead the team. There had been some talk that he did not have the right temperament for the job; but those of us who had played with him knew that Viv would be a determined captain, and that he had learned a great deal from his long stint as Lloyd's vice-captain. Furthermore, the most important legacy that Lloyd had left was a team in which any individual could have been chosen as captain without seriously affecting the cricket itself, although a decision to make any other member the captain would probably have brought doubts to the surface.

For their part, the New Zealanders portrayed the strategy they would adopt for the series from the first game: they would try to draw the tests and didn't care too much one way or the other how the limited overs games went. They succeeded in the first and second tests which were played on wickets so lifeless that it was surprising that anyone got out at all. I have always found it amazing that we are a team using a fast bowling attack ranked the best in the world, with batsmen capable of scoring runs off the opponents' quickies, yet the wickets in the West Indies are often slow and easy. I don't think that would happen in England or Australia if they had a team like ours.

In the first test at Trinidad, having given the New Zealanders 307 runs to win in four and a half sessions of the match, we failed to bowl them out, mainly because the pitch was slow and lacked bounce. In the second test at Guyana, 1,219 runs were scored for the loss of only twenty-one wickets. In the first innings, led by a stylish 185 from Richie Richardson and 90 from Haynes, we amassed 511 for 6 declared and then were ground into the Bourda dust as the New Zealanders made 440. Martin Crowe scored 188 before he was out lbw. By the time he got out, it was clear that the game would be drawn.

During the third test, I received news that, although expected, still broke me up. Gran had been taken ill and was in hospital. I left the Oval in a hurry and rushed to the hospital. I was deeply upset, and fought away the despression, but I couldn't fight away the tears. I felt as though a vacuum had developed inside my body that nothing or no one could ever fill again. I loved that old lady. I found comfort in my gratitude that the Old Man upstairs had made it possible for me to be able to provide her with a more comfortable life in her later years than she might otherwise have had. I was struck by a feeling of loneliness on entering the house I knew I would experience from that moment on whenever I came home. I would miss the conversations we used to have. I would miss her comradeship. I would miss her understanding and help. I would miss her love.

I phoned the Oval to be told that the game would start after I had taken my young cousin Bert to the hospital to see Gran we hurried back to the ground. I had missed my training. But the Captain and players understood my situation.

If we were going to beat the New Zealanders, Kensington would offer the best opportunity. The New Zealand team doubtless knew of our record at that ground. We had beaten India by an innings in 1976, Australia in 1978, England in 1981, and India and Australia in the previous two seasons. After the New Zealanders saw the wicket on the morning before the start of the test match, they must have had visions of their scalps being added to our collection.

The wicket was green and appeared lightning fast. In fact, the Kensington wicket played evenly; but you couldn't tell the New Zealand batsmen that. When they lost the toss and Viv Richards sent them in to bat, you could immediately sense their fear and insecurity. Heavy rains delayed the start and reduced playing time on the first day and yet our opponents lost 4 wickets for 18 runs off 19 overs.

After Marshall got Wright to touch the last ball of the first over to Dujon behind the stumps, Howarth pushed a short ball into Greenidge's hands at gully. From then on, the procession continued, broken only by stoppages for rain. The New Zealanders reached their total of 94 only because Logie dropped

Jeff Crowe when he had scored 1, and Hadlee batted determinedly for his high score of 29. The batsmen were obviously afraid of Marshall, bowling round the wicket; and their performance was not really what was expected of a test team.

Haynes and Richards soon showed them that the pitch hid no demons. The former made 62 and the skipper virtually mauled the bowling for 105, including a contemptuous six off Boock the last ball before lunch on the second day. Marshall then made 63 runs that confirmed him as an all-rounder of class, and I delighted in a brief knock of 37 not out. I took one thoroughly enjoyable six off Boock from an on-drive that sailed over the stands. We were all out for 336, a lead of 242 that more or less guaranteed Viv Richards his first win as captain of the side.

Although we were a bowler short since Holding had strained a muscle in his leg during the first innings, and the wicket was still easy-paced, the New Zealanders batted in the second innings only marginally better than they had done in the first. Expecting every ball to spit in their faces like a striking snake, they failed miserably against Marshall, who took 7 for 80 in the second innings to bring his tally in the match to 11 for 120. We bowled them out for 248, and the game only went into the final day because of fairly good efforts from Coney and Boock. They had avoided an innings defeat by seven runs. This gave the West Indies its first victory over New Zealand since 1969, thirteen tests earlier.

My departure to Jamaica was delayed by a day so that I could visit my gran. By then she had deteriorated so much that I told my aunt to prepare herself for the worst. She actually passed away on the first day of this test match – 4 May 1985.

There was no hope of New Zealand winning the series when we went to Jamaica for the fourth and final test match. The wicket on the first day was firm and the weather conditions good; but the New Zealanders, frozen in their defensive posture, sent us in to bat. Greenidge and Haynes put on 82 for the first wicket in spite of good restraining bowling from Hadlee, and when Haynes and Richardson added 62 more it looked as though we would put together a match-winning score. In the event, it took a stylishly controlled innings of 70 from Dujon, playing before his home crowd, and a little beauty of 26 from Marshall for us to reach 363 just after lunch on the second day.

The New Zealanders immediately found themselves in trouble before tea when they lost 3 wickets for 36 runs. After the interval, a shower delayed the resumption of play for more than an hour. I don't know what had happened during the delay, but when we came back to bowl on the pitch after tea on that second day, we found it a completely different stretch. In fact, it had become the kind of wicket that the New Zealanders had feared without experiencing. At the end of our innings, Hadlee had bowled six bouncers in an over at me. He had also bowled about four at Malcolm Marshall. It was clear to the two of us that something of the spirit of the last New Zealand tour had crept into the game. Now it was our turn. Rutherford ducked into a short-pitched one and was struck on the helmet. Coney was struck on his forearm which fractured. For eleven overs Marshall and I had them under intense pressure. Incredibly, with all the fireworks, we actually got only one wicket in that session: Rutherford caught behind in the last over of the day. I must admit, though, that we enjoyed delivering the goods to the New Zealanders after our ill-fated tour of 1980.

The New Zealanders must have been grateful for the rest day. On the fourth morning, the wicket had returned to its previous tame state; but our visitors didn't immediately seem to notice. I got one to skid through to hit Smith's off stump in the first over, with the batsman in no position at all to play the ball; but it was Davis, bowling an excellent line and length, who caused them the most problems. He took the last four wickets, and they were all out for 138.

Viv sent them back in to bat and I got Wright, the danger man of the first innings, when the score was 13. Slowly, however, the New Zealanders realized that most of the problems they had been experiencing were of their own making. On the sluggish wicket, Crowe and Howarth had little difficulty in managing whatever we bowled at them. By close, they were 78 and 108 not out respectively and New Zealand, at 211 for 1, were only fourteen runs away from making us bat again.

On the fourth day, Marshall and I decided to go for line and length on the easy-paced wicket. We slowed their run rate down to a dribble, before Richards came on himself to get Crowe for 112 with their score at 223. Often after long partnerships, when one batsman leaves the other soon follows. In the next over, Howarth attempted a flashing cut off Walsh and was caught in the gully. The response from my team-mates who gathered around confirmed that I had taken a blinder. Walsh then served up a near perfect bouncer to Martin Crowe that surprised the batsman by its wicked lift and pace, and he could only nick it to the wicket-keeper.

Without Coney, the New Zealanders had little chance of making sufficient runs to prevent us from winning, though the wicket continued to play easily. From 228 for 4, they crumbled to 283 all out. Marshall, bowling around the wicket, caused the most severe damage to their hopes by taking four of their last five wickets to bring his total for the series to twenty-seven, a new record. We needed only 58 runs to win, and I was packing my bags for home long before Greenidge and Haynes knocked them off to provide us with our seventh consecutive victory in a series at home.

The series against the New Zealanders was a thoroughly satisfying one from the point of view of our performance as a team. We had won every one-day international, and two out of the four tests. Perhaps we bowled with a bit more hostility than we would have done against another team, for we had not completely forgotten our 1980 experiences in New Zealand; but the New Zealand negative, defensive and sometimes frightened attitude was as responsible for their defeats as much as were our individual performances. Viv Richards had come through with flying colours during his first series as captain. There were no unsightly incidents off the field to spoil the cricket, such as it was.

At the end of it all, we were still a good team of seasoned professionals enjoying a run of success. I hope that the New Zealanders enjoyed their tour of the West Indies more than we had enjoyed our stay in their country in 1980. Had West Indian groundsmen travelled with us then, I don't think that the New Zealanders would have even completed the tour. But these things are all part of the life of a West Indian fast bowler: to work your guts out at home on wickets that favour the opposition.

16

My 1985 English summer season was marred by recurrent injury and so I was unable to play for Somerset as much as I would have liked. I returned to England late due to the burial of my grandmother on 11 May. I tried to come to terms with Gran's passing, but it wasn't easy lying in bed in Taunton with an injured knee and time to reflect on what her loss would mean to me. I read a great deal, listened to jazz, tried my hand at photography when I was mobile, and thought about the future. Once again, as seemed to happen each time I was injured, reports were circulating that my departure from the test scene was imminent. During the 1985 Shell Shield series in the Caribbean, a new generation of West Indian fast bowlers had come of age. I was quite taken aback to learn that I was being mentioned among the 'old stagers' whose days were numbered.

Nonetheless, I was certain that no newcomer would replace me in the team by bowling *only* as well as I could. Anyone seeking to replace me would need to have more ability than the 'Bird'; but I still remained concerned about my fitness. I kept nursing the knee and hoping that it wouldn't get worse. A short tour to Pakistan and Sharjah in the United Arab Emirates did nothing to improve my fitness. I caught bronchitis, lost a lot of weight, and generally felt that Pakistan might be a welcome place for others but it would never do for me. I had not enjoyed Pakistan on my previous visit and had agreed to the experimental tour mainly because, in the immortal words of one Malcolm Marshall, 'the mortgage has got to be paid somehow.'

On my return to England to help make arrangements for my benefit year in 1986, I got a phone call from a member of the Barbados Cricket Board of Control enquiring about my availability and interest in leading the Shell Shield team.

The Barbados team, the previous year's winners of the trophy and the winners overall more times than any other side, had had a disappointing season in 1985. They came second last. Never before beaten by an innings in Shield history, they had fallen by that margin to both Jamaica and Trinidad. The test players had not been available; but that was no real excuse for their performances. Nor was it a consolation regarding their prospects because the other teams would also be strengthened by the return of their test players. If I took on the captaincy, it would mean extra hard work just before the England tour of the Caribbean started. It seemed to me, nevertheless, that I owed it to Barbados to do all I could to help it regain the cricket respectability of which all Barbadians are proud. I accepted the offer and crossed my fingers that my physical fitness would withstand the added pressure. That I was to be captain gave me added incentive to get back into peak condition as quickly as possible.

Barbados managed to recapture the Shield, the most pleasurable games being those in which we beat Jamaica and the previous year's champions, Trinidad. We had secured the championship by the end of the fourth game, and only missed achieving the double because Malcolm Marshall decided to rest for the limited overs game against the Leeward Islands. Throughout the series, Marshall gave me the utmost support. He was not alone in this respect. Our test players, Greenidge, Haynes and Thelston Payne (reserve wicket-keeper), all played admirably in helping Barbados to re-establish its superiority. This does not mean that the younger players gave any less. Influenced by our professionalism and attention to detail, and willing to learn what the test players brought to the team, all of the younger players improved their game. The opening batsman, Carlisle Best, soon to be called up by the West Indies for his first test appearance, batted with ability and concentration throughout.

Best is a technically sound batsman with the temperament of Geoff Boycott, the same hunger for runs and desire to produce long innings. Unfortunately, these are not the only traits he shares with the stubborn Yorkshireman. With a change in his attitude towards his team-mates, Best will doubtless develop into an opener fully capable of replacing either Greenidge or Haynes in the West Indies squad.

The two main problems I encountered as captain of the

Barbados team concerned team selection. Because I wanted to give the youngsters a chance to experience play at a high level, and with an eye to the future, I had argued for the inclusion of new players. At times I had some difficulty getting the team that I wanted, and discovered that favouritism and short-sightedness still affected decisions concerning the selection of the Barbados team. I never got the teams I really wanted; but compromised with the other selectors' choices and did my best with what we put together.

The second problem was that I felt that I had to lead from the front to get the discipline and application I felt was necessary. As captain, I had to play in all of the games including the limited overs contests, and ended up bowling 141 overs in the Shield series for my twenty-eight wickets. Marshall missed a couple of games, but still managed to bowl 127 overs. At one stage it looked as if Barbados would win the Shell Shield at the expense of the West Indies team because two of its leading bowlers had accummulated between them over 250 overs in the weeks immediately preceding the first test against England.

Disruption threatened the 1986 English tour to the West Indies. England had recalled to their squad a number of players previously banned for sporting contacts with South Africa. English sports writers had climbed on to one of their favourite hobby horses and determined before the tour started that the return of Gooch and Emburey would make the England team stronger than the one we had soundly beaten in their last series against us. They said the team would be good enough to beat us in the Caribbean but the only real fear I harboured concerned demonstrators who promised to shatter the tour. The West Indian players who had joined rebel teams to tour South Africa in 1983 had been given life-bans, and some supporters in the Caribbean felt that it was unfair for Englishmen to play on grounds from which local players had been permanently banned.

Apart from the games against the Leeward Islands and Trinidad, the spectators for the most part ignored the demonstrators and turned out in high numbers for the matches. On the cricket field, the Englishmen immediately ran into trouble and the tone of the tour was established even before the first test was played. The tourists lost their opening encounter against the Windwards and barely managed to pull off a draw against the Leewards. In both games, they had faced neither devastating bowling nor a particularly wicked pitch, and yet their batting had shown surprising weaknesses that Marshall and co. were gleefully waiting to exploit.

We got our chance in the first one-day international played in Jamaica. England had boosted their confidence by winning against Jamaica; but not before Holding and Walsh had given them more than their fair share of discomfort. Omitted from the team and waiting in the wings, was Patrick Patterson who was built like a bull and who had been deadly on the Sabina Park wicket during the Shell Shield series. He opened the first limited overs game with an explosion. Sharing the new ball with me in the absence of the injured Holding, he spectacularly clean bowled Tim Robinson and had Gower caught in the slips before either had scored. Not even the new bowling machine that the English team had brought with them could have adequately prepared them for the fire Patterson lit at Sabina.

What happened next probably affected the English batting performance and the eventual outcome of the series more than any other single event. Mike Gatting, their vice-captain, taking the fight to Marshall, twice hooked for four. Marshall then bowled a short ball; but this time Gatting again went for the hook shot, which wasn't really on, missed the ball completely, and was struck in the face. We later learned that his nose had been broken and that he would have to miss most of the series. To add insult to injury, the ball that struck Gatting also fell on to his stumps. Gatting is a highly capable batsman and had been the only Englishman to show any true form. His absence left a gaping hole in the middle of their batting order.

Marshall went on to take three more wickets. I was quite satisfied to restrain the batsmen and pick up Downton and Emburey. Patterson had taken the other two wickets to fall. England made 145 for 8 off 46 overs. I gleaned as much information as I could from their innings. Gooch had batted steadily although he had given a chance to the slips off Patterson when on 11, and had gotten out to a late away-swinger from Marshall. Gower was flat-footed when he got out waving to a ball outside his off stump to give a catch to Richards at first slip. Willey and Lamb looked dangerous before getting out to catches in the deep. With the exception of Botham, who had been injured and did not play, and whom I knew well anyway, I had taken a look at the front-line English batsmen and had liked what I saw. Surely they were not going to be capable of the wonders against our attack that the English press had predicted.

We made the 146 runs required for victory for the loss of 4 wickets in 43 overs and five balls, in the process providing Greenidge, Haynes and Richardson with valuable batting practice against their bowlers. The ease of the victory was no surprise. I really had expected a greater fight from the tourists; but they had found Marshall and Patterson virtually unplayable. I was looking forward to the first test to see if that would remain the case.

It more or less did. After David Gower had won the toss and decided to bat on a wicket that was quite inconsistent in bounce, England, with the exception of Gooch and Lamb, succumbed meekly for 159 runs. Patterson, bowling very quickly and very straight, took 4 for 29. Marshall, Holding and I got two each. Yet, at the beginning of the innings, it looked as if they would make a far more challenging total. Robinson was defending courageously, Gooch was batting well, and the wicket provided us with very little help. Then Patterson was brought on, and in his third over he found the edge of Robinson's bat to provide Greenidge in the slips with a straightforward catch. Gower tried to hit himself into form before he was lbw to Holding. England were quickly 54 for 3 when David Smith, the newcomer, nibbled at a Patterson bouncer and Dujon hauled him in. The next seven wickets fell for 105 runs.

When we batted, Thomas bowled an extremely fast first over at Haynes that Dessie was lucky to survive; but then Greenidge got to face the youngster and gave him a father's correction with three admirably executed boundaries: an on drive, a cover drive and a blazing square cut. Proceedings were held up for a while when Greenidge complained about Edmonds fielding too close at bat pad. It appeared that the fielder was also trying to unnerve the batsman by talking to him while he tried to concentrate. I thought that we were about to be involved in a replay of the Australian tour when our domination drove the opposition to all sorts of gamesmanship and pranks; but Gower soon relieved the tension by moving Edmonds back. Greenidge continued to play aggressively, though needing a runner after he was struck on the knee by Ellison. Soon afterwards, he miscued a pull and was struck above the eye and had to leave the field. I replaced him as night-watchman and remained through to the close when we were 85 without loss.

On the second day, the English bowlers restrained us and we could manage only 268 for 7 by the close. I made what I considered a satisfactory 24 in over two hours batting and Gomes, his usual steady self, contributed 56. We had a lead of 109 runs. After we were all out for 307, Marshall and I smashed them. In my first over, I got one to keep low that knocked back Robinson's off stump. The following over, Marshall produced a beauty to clean bowl Gooch. Both English openers had departed for a duck. Lunch was taken with England on 18 for 2.

When play resumed, they lost five wickets for 103 runs as we rushed towards victory. Gower was completely outfoxed by Richards. In the first innings, the England captain had twice intentionally sliced Patterson over the slips for boundaries. Now, Richards positioned Best on the third man boundary and he took an excellent catch, running in to remove Gower who had attempted the same stroke when Patterson fed him the bouncer outside his off stump. After their captain departed, the Englishmen put up only token resistance. Willey, with his strange stance, stayed around for 71 runs. Botham, always aggressive in desperate situations, tried to swipe England out of trouble and managed 29 runs – 14 off one Marshall over – before Marshall fooled him into expecting a bouncer and instead produced a good length ball that struck his off stump with Botham perfectly positioned to pull or hook. England were 95 for 5, and it looked as though we would win by an innings when the ninth wicket fell at 146.

The last pair saved some of their wounded pride by forcing us to bat again to make the five runs required for victory when they were all out for 152. We had beaten them with two days to spare. The dream of some miraculous English revival after the return of the banned players was destroyed. But that match had been played in Jamaica. The second test was to be played in Trinidad, and, in the past, the wicket there had never really favoured fast bowling. With Emburey and Edmonds providing the more suitable spin, and their batting reinforced by the inclusion of Wilf Slack who had been called from the England B-team tour of Sri Lanka to replace Gatting, the Trinidad game did not promise to be the walk-over that the Jamaican one was.

My suspicions seemed warranted when in the one-day game immediately preceding the test, England not only won; but made 230 runs in 37 overs to do so. Never appearing to stand a chance until the last over, they pulled off one of the most stunning upsets in one-day cricket history. We made 229 for 3, thanks to two spectacular innings from Richards (82 off 39 balls) and Richardson (79 not out). When Botham opened the innings, it was clear that they had planned a chase. I thought that I had put a stop to that when I got Botham for 8 caught at mid-on.

I was shocked to find that some of the players blamed me for the defeat through my failure to contain the batting early on; but Slack provided admirable defence and Gooch played magnificently. If some of his strokes bordered on recklessness, this could be justified by the number of runs required. The two of them added 89 runs; but even at 98 for 2, there didn't seem to be cause for alarm. The rest was all Gooch. When the fifth wicket fell in the thirty-third over they still needed 47 runs; but he played with such brilliance that he had whittled that down to 9 from the last over, and finally 1 off the last ball which he got by scampering for a leg bye.

In winning the limited overs game, England – or rather, Gooch – had torn our bowling and had completely outplayed us. Marshall and I had given up 121 runs between us, Patterson had been hit for 30 off 6 overs and Harper for 22 off 3. It was not reassuring to know that, however our side for the test was chosen, the bowlers that had just been smashed all over Queen's Park would constitute its strike force.

Viv Richards won the toss and sent England in to bat. The visitors' first innings of the second test was played as if they wanted to prove that the display in the one-day game had been a mirage. We had included Barbadians Carlisle Best and Thelston Payne in the team, the latter because Dujon had broken a finger and the former because of his outstanding performances in the Shell Shield series. They were both soon in the game. Best took a catch to dismiss Gooch off Marshall for 2, and Payne took Slack behind the wicket off the same bowler for the same score. England were 11 for 2, and both of the batsmen who had caused the problems in the one-day match were back in the dressing room. They were soon 30 for 3 when Willey was caught behind off Patterson.

England recovered somewhat from these early shocks with a fourth wicket partnership of 78 to reach 108 for 3 by lunch. Gower's and Lamb's batting was admirably supported by some extremely wayward bowling. Patterson had trouble with his run-up, and at one stage was no-balled four times in an over. I knew from experience that this could have done nothing to improve his rhythm. His first five overs cost 44 runs. Walsh could get nothing out of the pitch and his first three overs cost 24. At lunch, we were collared, it looked like England might make a massive score. We had our usual chat and it was agreed that Marshall and I should resume after the interval.

After lunch, Gower played the wrong line to a faster one and was trapped lbw for 66. Botham then came to the crease and both Marshall and I knew that he would try to maintain the scoring rate that Gower and Lamb had established. We also knew that if we could contain him for any length of time – and a couple of overs for Botham is like an eternity – we could expect him to err. Surely enough, after he had scored 2, he lost his patience and edged Marshall to second slip and into the safe hands of Richie Richardson. The flow of the innings then turned dramatically. Only Lamb appeared confident. Emburey was caught behind for a duck, and later Marshall, diving and tumbling, came up with a wonderful catch in the slips to remove Lamb also off my bowling for 62. At tea and 163 for 8, England soon saw their earlier score of 136 for 3 transformed to 176 all out in the space of 19 overs. By the close, we had scored 67 and lost Greenidge.

The next morning, Haynes and Richardson, advised to start slowly and play themselves in so that we could try to reach a fairly reasonable score, followed instructions exactly. They added 150 runs, mostly off the fast bowlers with Greg Thomas and Ian Botham coming in for especial punishment. To prevent him from getting into a groove, Botham had to be manhandled. They took twenty-five runs off four of his overs and he had overall figures of 0 for 64 from 9 overs before lunch, when we had moved to 172 for one with Richardson 75 and Haynes 52.

After the interval, Richardson continued the onslaught. He was severe on Thomas, pummelling him with a hook for four, a straight drive for another four, and another hook for six off successive deliveries. The fast bowlers were out of it. When the spinners came on, it was quite a different story. Emburey and Edmonds perfectly exploited the slow Queen's Park wicket to reduce the scoring rate. Immediately after reaching his century, Richardson top edged a sweep off Emburey and was caught behind for 102. Haynes, unable to push the scoring along and heckled by the impatient spectators, tried to flick Emburey and was stumped for 67.

The crowd was unappreciative both of the spinners' ability and our need to grind them down. Some spectators slow-hand clapped and were perhaps responsible for both Gomes and Best getting out trying to force the pace against an accurate attack. Richards slammed a quick 34, almost everyone had a go, Marshall contributing a fine 22 not out when at the close we were 347 for 6, 171 runs ahead.

Our last two wickets made a further 52 runs before we were bowled out. We had a lead of 223. But that was no indication of how the match would end – since we had been held to draws in the previous three tests at Trinidad after having established good positions to win. In addition, the wicket had continued to play slowly during the morning session.

The Englishmen could blame neither the pitch nor particularly hostile bowling for the disastrous start to their second innings. Before he had scored, Slack pushed a straightforward delivery from me towards the vacant mid-off position and started for a run. Gooch did not respond and Slack was run out. They were 20 for 1 at lunch, and could have been in even deeper trouble had I taken a gentle chance offered by Gooch off Walsh.

Between lunch and tea, Richards kept Walsh and Patterson bowling. I thought that he was appreciative of the sluggishness of the wicket and the fact that Marshall and I had bowled a tremendous number of overs in the first innings. Gooch and Gower, the latter with a great deal of luck, tried to consolidate the English innings; but Walsh confused and bowled Gower with a ball that struck off stump after beating the batsman between bat and pad. He then removed Gooch lbw padding up to an inswinger. At tea, they were 109 for 3, and their chances of saving the game were slipping away.

After the interval, Marshall and I took over; and we might have broken the back of the innings if Marshall had held a comfortable chance at slip that Willey offered when he had scored 10. As it was, Willey and Lamb were still together when the umpires called play off because of fading light half an hour before the close. England were 168 for 3, and after the rest day, the fourth day promised to be a tense attempt of them trying to avoid defeat.

In the first session of the fourth day, Marshall and Walsh teamed up to demolish England's middle order. Walsh trapped Lamb lbw, and Marshall quickly removed Botham to a great catch behind, before he clean bowled Willey. Emburey and Downton quickly followed, and I finally got a wicket when Edmonds edged behind. It looked as if it was all over, with their score at 214 for 8; but Ellison and Thomas and Crickus combined to prevent an innings defeat. The last wicket pair added a record 72 runs before Ellison, after batting for more than three hours, was adjudged lbw to Marshall just before tea. By close of play, we had made 76 for the loss of Greenidge's wicket and needed only 17 more runs to chalk up a seventh straight win over England. No rain fell on the final morning, though two further wickets did, but we made the runs.

Because of the controversy surrounding the inclusion of players in the English side who had played in South Africa there was no test played in Guyana. The two to be played in Trinidad must have been the ones the Englishmen thought could offer their best chances of beating us, or at least securing a draw. Having batted so dismally on the first day, their chances of getting back into the game were progressively eroded and then finally wiped out by Malcolm Marshall. After this game, they seemed to lose some of their determination.

By the time the English team arrived in Barbados, the English reporters had begun a tirade against the team. Ian Botham, going through all kinds of problems on the field with both bat and ball, seemed specially picked upon by the vultures who masqueraded as scribes. He was accused of everything from attendance at drug parties to smoking marijuana while fielding in the slips. It was a truly disgusting display by journalists who could not understand why a team they had praised and thought had an excellent chance of beating us could be defeated so convincingly. The fact of the matter was that the English team had their chances, but for one reason or another they could never capitalize on them.

The reporters had singled out Botham, and hinted that his private life off the field was affecting his and the team's performance on it. Botham is a talented cricketer, with the temperament of the old West Indian calypso players. He is a strong competitor, and able in many departments of the game. In my opinion he has perhaps been fortunate to establish some of his cricketing records when he did. But I think he is unlucky to have played in the same county side as his pal, Viv Richards, whom he tries to emulate, in my opinion, to the detriment of the development of his own quite considerable gifts. About his extra-curricular exploits, nothing needs be said. A cricketer establishes himself on the playing field, and in the dressing room. A man is entitled to have a private life away from his profession.

The English team's run of miserable luck and poor performances continued in Barbados where they lost to the local team which I led. In the four-day game they were bowled out for 171 and 312 with Botham making a respectable 70 in the second innings. They were beaten by three wickets after giving us 267 runs to win. I had the pleasure of making the winning shot with three of the mandatory twenty overs remaining. That the Barbados side had played without Greenidge, Haynes and Marshall could have done nothing to build English confidence for the one-day international and third test. Nor would they have been encouraged when they learned that Gatting, having rejoined them only hours earlier from London after treatment for his broken nose, had broken his right thumb when he was struck there by Vibert Greene, the Barbadian medium pacer.

Gatting had made 36 solid runs, with the strokes of an in-form player who showed no signs of having had an enforced rest from the game. The ball that caused the injury had once again also taken his wicket.

We moved ahead 2–1 in the one-day series by beating

England by 135 runs. The visitors appeared completely demo-
ralized. Some of them would, apparently, have preferred to be
in some damp and foggy English town than in the blazing
sunshine of Barbados. Richards and Richardson both made 62
effortless runs to guarantee us the 249 we made for 7 off 46
overs. England were never in the game after Gooch was out
caught behind, early in their innings, and they formed a sad
procession as they were tumbled out for 114 in 39 overs. They
could not have been looking forward to the third test, nor
cheered by Viv Richards' assurance that we fully intended to
maintain the pressure. Viv said, 'We have played superior
cricket to have won the first two test matches of the current
series convincingly, and we will therefore approach the third
test full of confidence. But we would not attempt to under-
estimate the opposition since their team include a number of
fine players, and they are capable of gaining the upperhand if
pressure is not constantly applied.'

The following day, the pressure was applied in the form of a
ferocious innings of 150 not out by Richie Richardson. Timing
the ball exceedingly well, placing it between fielders with an
effortlessness that must have dismayed them and ably supported by a subdued Desmond Haynes who made 84, Richie
had capitalized on David Gower's decision to send us in to bat.
At the close of the first day we were 269 for 2. That night, the
English hotel rooms could not have been the scene of much
merriment, let alone the raucous parties of which some members
of their side were accused of attending.

Richardson added only twelve runs to his overnight total on
the second morning before he was lbw to the persistent
Emburey. By lunch, with our score 362 for 4 Richards was on
51 not out and looked ready to follow the scorch-marked path
that his fellow Antiguan had blazed out the previous day. The
feeling in the dressing room was that we would amass a truly
awesome total; but the first ball after lunch took Richards'
wicket and thereafter we collapsed for 418 runs. That the fast
bowler Greg Thomas had done the most severe damage with
figures of 4 for 14 off 6 overs must have been something of a
mixed blessing for the English batsmen who then had to pad
up to face our four quickies.

As frequently happened during the series, England had a

disappointing start. With the score at 6, Robinson tried to hook Marshall and only succeeded in helping the ball through to Dujon. Thereafter, for the rest of the day, Gower and Gooch exploited our short-pitched bowling to lift their score to 110 for 1 and their hopes high.

On the third day, however, once again the importance of a fine stand by two of the English batsmen was completely wiped out by the inadequate play of the others. The wicket had a new-found venom; and though the bounce became increasingly uneven, there was nothing in it to prevent a careful batsman from getting some runs. None of them did.

Gower touched a Marshall outswinger to the wicket-keeper, and Gooch was to follow suit. They were 3 for 134. An hour after lunch, they were all out for a miserable 189. Sent back in to bat 229 runs in arrears, things never got better for them, and they folded to 132 for 6 by the close. It was a suicidal display, with batsmen using almost precisely the opposite tactics to those that might reasonably have been expected to work. Botham, for example, tried to fight fire with fire and flashed away for twenty-one runs when he might have taken a more cautious approach on a wicket where one could not have known how high the next ball would bounce. (This is not a criticism, however, for I can remember Both doing this on more than one occasion and pulling his team out of the fire and putting them into winning positions.) When he finally pushed forward uncertainly to an outswinger on the second ball of the day's final over and became wicket-keeper Dujon's fifth catch of the day, it was all over for England bar the shouting. Ten minutes before lunch on the fourth day, the shouting could begin. It took that long only because twenty minutes were lost to rain and Emburey and Downton put up stubborn resistance. We bowled them out for 199 and had won by an innings and 30 runs. I had captured 4 for 69 and was pleased as punch by that, and by the fact that we had secured the series.

Back in Port-of-Spain for the one-day match, Viv Richards won the toss and put England in to bat. They set about their innings as if it was a chore with which they would rather have nothing to do. Graham Gooch began the decline by gently turning an innocuous short-pitched delivery from Marshall straight to

Richards at mid-wicket when their score was 15. Robinson and Gower then shared a long partnership; but the way they went about it was more in the style of batsmen seeking practice, or playing in a five-day game, then of men who knew that run-rate was all-important. By the time Robinson was fourth out, splendidly yorked by Marshall with the score at 126, there was little doubt that we would win the game. After he left, only Botham, before he lifted a dolly to Harper at mid-wicket off my bowling when he had made 29, showed any appreciation of the nature of the one-day game. I clean bowled Ellison and Edmonds with the last two balls of the innings to bring the English misery to an end. They had made 165 for the loss of 9 wickets off 47 overs.

In our turn to bat, Greenidge was quickly bowled by Foster for a duck; but Haynes and Richardson added 75 before the latter was caught by Gooch off Embury. Viv Richards then revelled in the situation to score 50 savage runs, including the winning hit to the cover boundary off Gower, and Haynes remained for 77 not out to secure victory for us by eight wickets. I was awarded the Man of the Match prize for my 3 for 22 off 9 overs; but it could just as easily have gone to Marshall, Haynes or Richards.

Had the English team packed their bags and departed the Caribbean after the fourth limited overs game, as reports had it that Graham Gooch wanted to do, I would not have been surprised. Winning against them was the only thing that we were interested in, that was the aim: to win at all costs. They simply did not handle our fast bowling attack; nor did they get our batsmen out for low scores.

On the Trinidad wicket, the English team got themselves into all kinds of trouble on the first day of the fourth test after they were sent in to bat. For about the first hour the wicket had some bounce in it; but in that time I was able to remove Gooch, Robinson and Gower for 19 runs in 8 overs, all caught off the outside edge. Smith and Lamb then put up something of a fight until lunch. Afterwards, first Patterson and then Holding accounted for the two of them. Botham, playing an innings distinctly out of character, made a painstaking 38 runs and saved his side from greater embarrassment. England were eventually all out for an even 200; I managed figures of 4 for

43. Greenidge and Haynes opened the innings for the West Indies and collected 12 runs before the end of the day's play.

On the second day, we made 271 for the loss of 7 wickets, due mainly to a fine 87 from Richards who brought a completely different complexion to the game. Gomes batted well in front of his home crowd scoring 48, and Greenidge made a sound 42. Emburey exploited the Trinidad wicket – as he had done in the second test – to restrict our scoring while taking three important wickets.

On the third day, we lost our last three wickets to Botham for the addition of forty-one runs and were 312 all out. England's batsmen, 112 runs behind, then undermined all Botham's good work by losing 3 wickets for 30 runs. Gooch went before a run was scored, hooking at Marshall's third ball and giving an easy catch to Dujon. Robinson on the back foot couldn't get his bat down quickly enough and was bowled. Gower did not play a shot to a Patterson delivery he expected to lift, and was out lbw. Apart from Smith (32) and Botham (25), the rest of the their innings was a shambles. They were all gone for 150 and we needed only 39 runs to win. By this time, the Trinidadian crowd were chanting the chorus of the most recent calypso, 'Captain, the ship is sinking.' By the time Greenidge and Hayes had knocked off these runs in five overs, they were singing, 'Oh dear, what can the matter be?'

I couldn't pretend to feel sorry for England. After all, pressure had a lot to do with their plight and they hardly ever had good starts.

By the time that England had been unceremoniously beaten by ten wickets with more than two days to spare at Queen's Park, everyone following the series expected us to complete a second straight clean sweep against them. This is the price that you pay for being successful. Every time you walk on to the field you are expected to win; no one is supposed to put up any opposition, and sometimes you pay dearly for success.

The fifth test was more or less decided on the first day. Desmond Haynes batted all day for 117 not out and we were 228 for 4 at close. On the second day, we piled up 474 runs before our innings came to an end. One indication of England's despondency was that Haynes added only 12 to his overnight score and Richardson, Gomes, Richards and Dujon all got out in the twenties. Marshall and Holding each played an exhilarating innings of **76** and **73**, respectively. Roger Harper got **60**, and I was run out for **11** trying to help Holding reach his half century. Our last four wickets had added **193** runs at much better than even time; the depression among the English players was clearly visible.

Beginning the third day at **40** without loss, England set about redeeming themselves with an opening stand of **127** that took up the whole first period. The St John's wicket was as quiet as a sleeping child. In our efforts to get something out of it, we constantly overstepped the popping crease, with the result that at the end of the day we had bowled **34** no-balls – **9** each from Marshall and Patterson and **8** each from Holding and me. The easy pace of the wicket brought nothing but frustration, and we were therefore dismayed when the umpires on two occasions exchanged softened and mis-shaped balls for soft, mis-shaped ones of a different brand. It's one thing to bowl on a featherbed. It's another to do so with a tennis ball.

Holding finally managed to dislodge Gooch lbw about half an hour after lunch when the Englishmen had scored **127**. Patterson accounted for Slack caught at shortleg off the very first ball of the next over. Almost predictably, the English middle order collapsed and they were **263** for **7** at the close. Gatting, warmly welcomed back to the tour after his misfortunes, had made **15** before he was caught behind by Dujon. David Gower was still there, on **70**; but he would not have been had I taken a relatively straightforward catch at gully off Holding just before the close. For one of the very few times in a test match, my mind had been wandering.

I had been totally surprised that the two Antiguans, Richards and Richardson, made only **50** runs between them in our first innings. After we had dismissed England for **310**, with Gower failing by ten runs to reach his century, one of them played more as I had anticipated. Viv Richards devastated the English bowling for **6** sixes and **7** fours in a century made off **56** deliveries. The way he was going I was glad that it was Botham and company bowling against him and not our side. When he mercifully declared our innings closed at **246** for **2**, Haynes had been run out for an excellently played **70**; but everyone at the

Recreation Ground had been astonished by the audacity of the innings.

Still in a state of shell-shock and requiring 410 runs to win, the dazed Englishmen lost Slack clean bowled and then Robinson, run out in an effort that perfectly reflected their level of bewilderment.

The next day, which everyone knew would be the last day, Gooch and Ellison, the night-watchman, stubbornly withstood our efforts to break through the middle order until just before lunch when Ellison was out lbw. With the crowd loudly singing 'Captain, the ship is sinking,' and Gower steadfastly refusing to accept the fact, we plugged away at him for almost an hour. When he finally departed, his head hung low like one finally forced to accept the inevitable, one over remained before the mandatory final twenty. The last pair, Downton and Foster, stood on the burning bridge for half an hour before Richards called for the second new ball and Malcolm Marshall. The flames of ten straight wins and two straight 'black-washes', as the banners declared, licked up and over the English last innings and eventually enveloped it taking it into Caribbean cricket history. They were 170 all out and we had a West Indian victory by 240 runs.

Both Marshall and I had taken twenty-seven wickets in the series, a new record for the West Indies in a home series against England. Marshall was made Man of the Series, deservedly so, I thought, because he had also contributed magnificently with the bat at times when the team needed it most. I was mentally tired after one of the hardest working summers I've ever had. Until the Antiguan test was over I hadn't realized what a toll the cumulative effects of playing in every first-class match had taken on me. Instead of the euphoria I would normally have experienced at the kind of success we had just achieved. I felt exhausted and empty and wanted to get back to Enterprise and to Gran; until I remembered that the kind old lady was there no more...

POSTSCRIPT:

The Summer Set Blues

The taste of West Indian success against the touring English team was soured when I discovered that Viv Richards and I were to leave Somerset at the end of the 1986 season. At the time, I didn't think that there was much that needed to be said about what was going on. We are professional cricketers, working under contract, and employers always retain the right to discontinue the services of those they feel no longer perform up to an expected standard. I suppose that would be the Somerset position. Events leading up to the decision, however, led me to a quite different appreciation of the situation.

I have not really wanted to talk about the more disenchanting aspects of my stay with Somerset. On the whole, I enjoyed playing with the club and honestly feel that I gave of my best. The surprise that my services were no longer required came after I had finished the draft of this book; and I knew that the text would end in anticlimax if I said nothing about the Somerset interlude. I thought about the best way of doing this and decided that a 'self-interview' would be the best way of presenting my point of view.

The interview was conducted in Enterprise, Christ Church, Barbados where I was relaxed and waiting to be recalled to the West Indian side for the 1986–7 tour of Australia. The West Indian Cricket Board of Control had quite generously agreed that Mikey Holding and I could miss the tour of Pakistan because we were tired; and neither of us wanted to subject our bodies, especially our stomachs, to another Pakistani experience. Joel Garner asked the questions and 'Big Bird' answered them. I reflected upon Somerset, and cricket, and a couple of other things. It is true: he knows nothing about cricket that only cricket knows.

Joel Garner: Bird, how do you feel about the Somerset decision not to renew your contract after the 1985 season?

Big Bird: Disappointment. I figured that Viv and I had contributed so much to the club that they would have given us the benefit of the doubt in any decision they felt they had to take. But then again, time is an ocean. It ends at the shore. You may not see me tomorrow.

Joel Garner: What does that mean?

Big Bird: It means that even things that appear unlimited, or infinite, or would last forever must come to an end. It wasn't so much the sacking that bothered me; but the way that it was done. It bothered me that people with whom I had worked and played, and for whom I was always prepared to go that extra mile, could treat me in such an unceremonious fashion. Some of them even went so far as to suggest that I did not always give of my best; and they themselves know that that's a lie. A damned lie.

Joel Garner: What, in your opinion, caused the Somerset authorities to come to the conclusions that they did? Surely, the fact that you and Viv Richards could not get the backing you needed in a special meeting of the membership meant that there was something to the club's position?

Big Bird: Well, there are really two questions involved there. One has to do with the strength of the club's position, and the other has to do with this whole thing about Viv Richards and Joel Garner. I've already said that the club's position doesn't really have anything to do with me. I was their employee and they had every right to discontinue my services whenever they felt like it. I was only worried about learning of my sacking from a radio sports report. I thought that they owed me more than that. Then there's this thing about Viv and Joel. God, in the summer of 1985 it had become something of a joke. I mean Laurel and Hardy, Martin and Lewis, Tracey and Hepburn,

Fish and Chips, Viv Richards and Joel Garner. The club more or less successfully tried to establish in people's minds that Joel Garner had the same personality as Viv Richards. By suggesting that the reasons for firing Joel Garner, whatever they might be, would be the same as those for firing Viv Richards. I don't want to appear to be dissociating myself from Viv; but anyone who knows the two of us would know that this Richards and Garner thing had just gotten out of hand. The aspect to it that would perhaps make sense would not flatter the Somerset crowd. These presumably intelligent people got rid of a world-class bowler and the best batsman in the world for a Crowe. In anybody's book, that's a joke.

Joel Garner: What about the charges that the two of you were disruptive influences on the team, that the overseas players were unable to mix with the English players, and that you tried to mix only rarely?

Big Bird: Quite frankly, that's a lot of hogwash. They said that they were trying to build a team and that Viv and I were too arrogant to mix. I don't think that I've ever been called arrogant before. The fact of the matter is that the arrogance at Somerset came more from another clique in the side than it did from the overseas players. Everyone forgot that the thing was about playing cricket. As far as building a team was concerned the coach should have been doing his job. The overseas players didn't stop him from doing his job. The whole thing was about image anyway.

Some people see a tri-coloured sweat-band on a fellow's wrist and all of a sudden he's a lunatic radical Rasta with a licence to kill. They succeeded in building up this image of Viv Richards' influence on Botham; so that when Both had his problems with the media during the West Indies tour, it would look like Viv Richards and the

West Indians were making a mess of the blue-eyed blond. But Botham is his own man. They forgot that. Somewhere behind the committee's decision lies the feeling that if they got rid of Richards and Garner the Botham problem would go away. Well it did; but not in the way that they thought it would.

Joel Garner: What about this whole thing about drugs? What is this Botham problem anyway?

Big Bird: Drugs are now a part of English life. The whole problem of drugs and the problem of image are related. Here again, when a fellow wears a tri-coloured sweat-band, he's supposed to be sending out a signal that he smokes marijuana, or at least condones the smoking of it. I don't have anything to do with drugs. Never have and never will. Botham said that he used to smoke and he nearly got crucified for saying so. I think that, at least in part, his whole debacle that summer was responsible for our dismissal.

Joel Garner: How? Surely you can't be saying that the committee fired you and Viv Richards because Ian Botham had a problem?

Big Bird: No, not really. It was just part of the whole scenario. It allowed it to become possible. But there were people at Somerset who had wanted to get rid of Richards and Garner for some time. I sensed it; but I don't think that Viv did until the very end. I remember when I called him up to tell him that we had been fired, he kept saying 'you'. He couldn't believe that he had been let go, too. He was livid. He kept saying, 'but, Bird, you don't sack your best bowler.' I had to remind him that you don't sack you best batsman either. He saw it as personal. He was as angry as he had been when Michael Hill had asked him in the dressing room one day whether he wasn't perhaps a little tired. Viv got the hint when Michael Hill went on to say that Martin Crowe would like to know what his position was at Somerset. Richards blasted him. He shouted, 'I put up these four walls and you come asking me shit about Martin Crowe?'

Joel Garner: So what does the whole issue mean for West Indian cricketers in English county cricket?

Big Bird: It's a clear warning. If two of the best players in the world can be sacked at their peak, it tells the younger lads: 'We don't care how good you are or what ability or promise you have. You are dispensable.' It should speak volumes, not only to the overseas West Indian professionals, but also to men like Cowans, Slack, Small, Butcher, and others like Mark Alleyne now coming along. The whole establishment of English cricket seems about to fight a rearguard action against certain players maintaining permanent places at the top. Look at Cowans. I've seen situations where he took eight wickets in a match and then be refused the new ball for the following game. Radio announcers and some old-fashioned nationalists are also involved. They tell the fans what they feel they ought to hear, not what is actually happening. There has been little praise for West Indian cricket over the past ten years. Constant criticism. Short-pitched bowling and slowing down the game, and a bunch of other rubbish. If the English or Australian team had experienced the same level of success, you would read and hear words like dynasty and comparison with history's best. Not in our case. There was a jealousy and selfishness among English players and commentators. At Somerset, the clique was always talking about the success of West Indies cricket and comparing it with any failure Somerset met. What they failed to realize was, for example, that I had three or four of the world's best bowlers with me for the West Indies. Playing for Somerset, I could be blocked out by the opponents for an hour. There isn't any point in players doing that against the West Indies. I've played in three-day games for Somerset when we had teams on the run at 20 for 2 in the first hour, and then they hold me and go to 140 for 2. I didn't have Macco Marshall at the other end. But the commentators and the intellectuals would say that I was not performing. Part of my disappointment at Somerset came from recognizing that they would never bring on any new young bowlers as long as I was there. The coaching was so bad you couldn't be blamed for thinking that it didn't exist.

Joel Garner: In what ways was it bad?

Big Bird: It was particularly bad in the area of man-management. The ability to get through to people without referring constantly to self or the past. The coach there always said things like 'in my day'. Cricket has changed a lot since his day. If some idiot thinks that I am going to bring the ball up to a batsman and have him drive past my close fielders and tire them out from chasing drives all day, he's crazy. Not when I can hold back a couple and have him fence to short-leg. Cricket has changed a lot. People don't stand around and applaud an opponent's good stroke, no matter how brilliant it is. They chase the ball. All that talk about 'in my day' is transparent nonsense. If the present West Indian attack had to bowl at May and Cowdrey, the English record books might look a lot different, although they were great players. As it was, in my opinion, the coach with his 'I', 'my' and 'in my day' failed to bring out the best in his players. He ended up with a team no better than any in our First Division in Barbados.

Joel Garner: Let's get back to the point about your sacking at Somerset. How good is Martin Crowe, your replacement? Have you ever played against him, and what is he like?

Big Bird: I don't know him personally. It was reported that he's said some strange things about what happened at Somerset; but he's entitled to his opinion. He didn't make the decision. I only know that we played against him in the West Indies and he made 179 on a mattress in Guyana and about 214 for the whole series, and this was pointed out by one of the players.

Joel Garner: How long had the storm been brewing?

Big Bird: The team spirit in the Somerset dressing room had been deteriorating for a couple of years. Nigel Poppingwell said he wrote to the President about it in 1984, but nothing was said before the Extra-ordinary General Meeting. But you have to remember that Somerset has a tarnished record as far as its treatment of its players is concerned. The ex-Chairman, Brian Langford, sacked Somer-set's most successful player. Said he couldn't play; but two senior players knew that Brian Rose was a good cricketer and worked on him. They also got rid of Roy Kerslake who was extremely close to the players. A good man-manager. A precedent that it might have done Viv and me good to have kept in mind was that Somerset got rid of Hallam and Moseley after twelve or so years with the same absence of cer-emony that they have shown in our case.

Joel Garner: Whom do you hold most responsible for the decision to fire you?

Big Bird: Peter Roebuck. A man who lacks sensitivity and good sense. I've never met a man who's read so much and knows so little. He was one of the persons most responsible for the myth of the overseas players disrupting the dressing room. I myself thought that there were other more disruptive influences in the dressing room than whatever vanity or arrogance his mind perceived. The captain was the disruptive influence; but the fellows were strong. He would go missing for days and nobody said anything about it. He is an incredibly moody man; but we accepted him as he was. Because one man had his moods, it didn't mean that we all had to be foolish. He's representative of the kind of mediocrity that is the real threat to English cricket. He's representative of that force in English cricket that is seeking to drag down others in order to accommodate itself instead of raising standards. They hate people with strong views or bold ideas. Everything you do or say can't be right. There must be contradiction. I've never agreed with everything that I've seen go on around me in a dressing room. If by being disruptive they mean not agreeing, then I'm guilty. I remember bowling for about an hour in one game with Herbie Dredge at the other end and our captain called Dredgie back when it was clear to everybody that the man was dead tired. I argued for the ball and he looked foolish in front of the other players. The next day the press reported that I bowled reluctantly. We had bowled the team out and won the game, and he never said a word to the press about what really happened.

I can't really be bothered about Roebuck. I feel sorry for him. At the end of the day, the man who's captain carries the burden; but the success of the team is more important even than he. If I'm your best bowler and you tell the groundsman to shave the wicket or make it white, it means that you don't give a damn about your bowlers. And wickets have been shaved on more than one occasion. If we're playing against Surrey, for example, and Sylvester Clarke happens to be playing, the wicket would be shaved to accommodate Sylvester Clarke rather than left green to accommodate Joel Garner.

Joel Garner: What other disruptive influences can you mention?

Big Bird: Don't ask me, ask the newspapers.

Joel Garner: What now, big man?

Big Bird: I'll be going to Australia with the West Indies side where I will be bowling my heart out once again. I'll play for Oldham in the League in England next year. After that, it all depends on my fitness and how I feel about this carousel that cricket has become. I gave of my best for all the teams I played with. I have nothing to be ashamed about. When I leave cricket, I will do so with my head high. Let me just share with you the Somerset chairman's final letter to me.

Dear Joel:

Now that the Special General Meeting has taken place, I would like to thank you for all that you have done for Somerset County Cricket Club since you joined the club in 1977. Your name will always be associated with the winning of our first trophies and with the invaluable contributions you made to our bowling. Above all, though, you will be remembered for your kindliness and friendliness to the Somerset fans and for the way that you never refused an autograph to the youngsters. I am very sad, we all are, that your departure from Somerset should have been so acrimonious. You did not deserve that fate, nor should you have been coupled with Viv and Ian for being disruptive in the dressing room.

On a personal note, I would like to thank you for all you have done for me. In spite of all that has happened I hope our friendship may continue over the years and I am delighted that you have obtained a post with Oldham.

You will always be welcome in Somerset and at the County Ground although I can understand if you do not wish to return whilst the present committee is still in office. One day when the dust has settled, I know the club would like to honour you in some way.

We wish you every success in your future career.

Yours sincerely

Michael

M. F. Hill, Chairman

As I was saying at the beginning, time is an ocean; but it ends at the shore.